W9-AUZ-956

Keep Your Stern Drive Running

Richard Thiel

International Marine
Camden, Maine

*To my father, who kept nagging me to follow directions
and pick up my tools.*

Published by International Marine
10   9   8   7   6   5   4   3   2   1
Copyright © 1992 International Marine, an imprint of TAB Books.
TAB Books is a division of McGraw-Hill, Inc.

Library of Congress Cataloging-in-Publication Data
Thiel, Richard, 1945–
   Keep your stern drive running / Richard Thiel
      p.   cm.
   Includes index.
   ISBN 0-87742-327-X
   1. Inboard-outboard engines—Maintenance and repair.   I. Title.
VM771.T45   1992
623.8'7234'0288—dc20   92-13787
                                  CIP

Questions regarding the content of this book should be addressed to:

International Marine
P.O. Box 220
Camden, ME 04843

Text design by Faith Hague, Watermark Design, Camden, Maine.

CONTENTS

Introduction   iv

Part One: How the Gasoline Stern Drive Works

1: The Internal Combustion Engine   2
2: How the Four-Cycle Gasoline Engine Works   6
3: The Fuel System   9
4: The Ignition System   15
5: The Cooling System   19
6: The Exhaust System   22
7: The Lubrication System   25
8: The Stern Drive Propulsion System   27

Part Two: How to Operate Your Stern Drive

9: The Log   38
10: The Daily Checklist   43
11: The Periodic Checklist   47
12: From Start-Up to Shutdown   54

Part Three: How to Care for Your Stern Drive

13: Selecting and Changing Oil   60
14: Caring for Fuel   64
15: Caring for the Ignition System   67
16: Doing It Yourself   70
17: How to Choose and Deal with a Mechanic   75
18: Basic Tools and Spare Parts   78
19: Basic Engine Troubleshooting   82

Index   87

Introduction

The purpose of this book is to give you a brief and painless explanation of how your gasoline-powered stern drive propulsion system works, plus provide some simple guidelines for operation and care of it so you will get maximum life and durability from it. Once you understand the basics provided here, you'll be able to devise your own operating and maintenance programs and deal intelligently with a mechanic when you need one.

This book is written for someone who knows absolutely nothing about engines and things mechanical and, equally important, someone who has little or no interest in them other than making sure they serve him or her well. In short, this is a basic survival manual for the owner of a boat that is equipped with a gasoline-powered stern drive.

This book is not about the history of stern drive development, how to conduct major repairs, or how to rebuild an engine or drive in your bedroom with just a hammer and a screwdriver. In fact, you'll find few, if any, references to actual repair procedures here. Instead the emphasis is on getting the best use out of your stern drive and preventing problems from occurring in the first place.

Why? Because in spite of what you may have read or heard to the contrary, the modern stern drive propulsion system is a complex piece of machinery. Unless you are a person of exceptional mechanical ability and have access to a large assortment of specialized tools, you will be far better off leaving significant repairs to someone who has the extensive specialized training in the art—yes, art—of troubleshooting and repairing a stern drive propulsion system.

Besides, the four-cycle marine engine is a very reliable engine, thanks principally to its automotive heritage. Indeed most stern drive engines are direct derivatives of automotive engines. The drive unit portion of this propulsion system is also reliable and in most cases is an adaptation of the well-proven outboard. If you operate and maintain your gasoline-powered stern drive properly, you should have years of trouble-free operation before you ever need to call a mechanic.

In addition to learning the basics of engine and drive operation, this book will help you choose the spare parts and tools that you should have aboard at all times. While you need only a few of each, having the right ones on hand can make the difference between a cruise that leaves you with fond memories and one that leaves only woeful regrets.

Finally, this book will provide you with a basic introduction to the art of troubleshooting, a skill you need to fix minor problems and to deal intelligently with the person you hire to fix the big ones. By applying the principles of troubleshooting and the basic working knowledge of the stern drive power system you will glean from the first chapters, you will—believe it or not—be able to reason through most maladies before having to call an expert.

Marine engines and drive systems represent the largest part of a boat's total cost—as much as half the cost of the boat when new, even more on a used boat. A good marine mechanic, if you can find one, typically charges $40 an hour and more—and it takes a lot of time to work on a boat. Add to that the fact that marine parts cost at least half-again as much as comparable automotive parts and you have good reasons to get as much trouble-free performance out of your propulsion system as you can.

Don't be alarmed by the bad news; there is good news too. If properly operated and maintained, the typical gasoline-powered stern drive can last as long as the boat into which it was installed. Consider that a well-maintained automotive gasoline engine lasts 100,000 miles, or roughly 2,900 hours, and that the average boat owner logs less than 200 hours on his or her boat each year. You can see that 10 years of life before major engine work is a realistic possibility. Drive systems are at least as durable. The key is making sure that you minimize wear by operating and maintaining your boat properly.

Giving you a working knowledge that allows you to maximize the trouble-free life of your gasoline-powered stern drive is what this book is all about.

 **PART ONE**

How the Gasoline Stern DriveWorks

The Internal Combustion Engine

The gasoline engine that powers your stern drive boat is basically identical to that under the hood of your car, with the exception of its cooling and exhaust systems. Like the marine diesel and the outboard, it is an **internal combustion engine**, so termed because it burns fuel inside itself to produce power as opposed to an **external combustion engine**, such as a steam engine, that burns fuel outside itself. The following description applies generally to all three kinds of marine internal combustion engines—the stern drive, the outboard, and the diesel.

The Basic Parts

The basic component of an internal combustion engine is the **engine block**, basically a chunk of metal (in stern drives, almost always cast iron) into which **cylinders** have been drilled. The cylinders may be configured in a single row, in which case the engine is called an **in-line**, or they may be arranged in two rows separated by anywhere from 60° to 90°, in which case the engine is called a **V**. Thus, if both kinds of engines had six cylinders, one would be called an in-line six and the other would be called a V-6.

Inside each cylinder is a **piston**, a slug of metal (usually aluminum) slightly smaller than the cylinder so it can slide up and down. The piston typically contains three grooves around its circumference near the top into which fit resilient metal **piston rings**. These rings press up against the walls of the cylinders, creating a tight seal.

Onto the top of the block (or more accurately, onto the top of each bank of cylinders) bolts another slug of cast metal (either iron or aluminum). When this metal cap, called the **cylinder head**, is in place, it leaves a small, sealed space in the cylinder between itself and the top

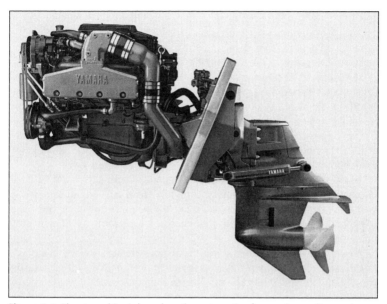

Figure 1-1 The stern drive is based on the automotive four-cycle gasoline engine. (Courtesy Yamaha)

of the piston. This space is known as the **combustion chamber**. Between the cylinder head and the block is a resilient metal/fiber **gasket** that ensures a tight seal. Although the piston moves up and down the cylinder, it never travels all the way to the top and touches the cylinder head; there is always a small area left between piston and cylinder head, and this is where fuel is burned to produce power.

Compression in a Gasoline Engine

If you were to measure the volume of the combustion chamber when the piston is at the bottom of its travel and compare it with the volume when the piston is at the top of its travel, you would come up with a pair of numbers called the **compression ratio**. For instance, in an engine with a nine-to-one (written 9:1) compression ratio each piston leaves nine times more volume when it's at the bottom of its travel than when it's at the top.

Whether we're speaking of a fireplace or a boat engine, the object is the same: to produce heat through the burning or combustion of fuel. All combustion requires three things: fuel, oxygen, and heat. In your fireplace, that usually means wood, room air, and a match.

To make combustion occur in an internal combustion engine we need to admit fuel—gasoline, in the case of the stern drive engine—

and fresh air into the combustion chamber. Once both are there in the proper proportion, we then must supply a heat source to ignite the mixture. In a gasoline engine that source is an electrical spark jumping between the poles or electrodes of a **spark plug**.

If you were to place a small amount of gasoline in a bowl in the presence of fresh, oxygenated air and touch a match to it, you'd get rapid combustion. (Take my word; please don't try it.) The gasoline near the surface would burn first and relatively quickly, but that below the surface would take longer, or might not even burn at all if the fresh air in the immediate vicinity were consumed. The process would generate some heat that theoretically could perform some work.

But if you took the same amount of gasoline and sprayed it into the air so that each droplet was surrounded by fresh air—in other words, if you **atomized** the gasoline—you'd get much more uniform and complete combustion. More complete combustion produces significantly more heat per unit of fuel.

Now, imagine spraying a mixture of gasoline and air inside a cylinder when the piston is roughly at the bottom of its travel, then sealing the space, and squeezing the mixture to, say, one-ninth its original volume. This time when you ignited it you'd produce even more heat out of the same fuel and you'd have done it more quickly and completely.

But you'd have to be careful, because when you compress air, you raise its temperature. If you squeeze a mixture of gasoline and air too much, it will ignite prematurely due to the heat generated by compression. The fuel/air mixture will explode while the piston is still traveling upward, causing a major collision and a loud bang or knock. If the collision, technically called **detonation**, is too severe, it can actually blow a hole right through the top of the piston.

Oil companies put additives in gasoline to make it resist such spontaneous ignition, an ability that is reflected in a gasoline's octane rating. But even with high-octane gasoline, 11:1 is about the highest compression ratio possible in a four-cycle gasoline engine without causing damage.

The Rest of the Story

The heat produced in an engine's combustion chamber generates **expansion**, forcing the piston down the cylinder. Each piston also has a horizontal shaft running through its center onto which clamps the smaller end of a **connecting rod**. The other, larger end of the connecting rod clamps to the arm of a **crankshaft**. Since both ends contain bearings that allow the rod to pivot, the crankshaft translates the vertical motion of the piston into rotary motion that can turn a wheel, generator, pump, or propeller. In multiple-cylinder engines, the crankshaft arms are at different angles, allowing each piston to reach the top of its cylinder at a different time, producing regularly spaced combustion and smoother running.

To make any engine last, two things must be controlled: friction and heat. Too much of either will destroy an engine. To control heat, blocks and cylinder heads are cast with internal passages through which liquid is circulated by an engine-driven **pump**. In your car, the coolant is routed to the radiator where air passing over its fins dissipates heat. A stern drive usually circulates the virtually unlimited supply of relatively cool water in which the boat floats.

You may think that the more heat a **cooling system** removes from an engine the better, but this isn't so. Remember that the purpose of the entire internal combustion process is to generate heat that can be put to work. If an engine runs too cold, the walls of the combustion chamber will cool, or **quench**, the expanding gases, producing incomplete combustion and less expansion and power.

Temperature is typically more important in a diesel engine than in a gasoline engine, since a diesel depends solely upon the heat generated by compression to ignite its fuel. Even in a relatively "cool" gasoline combustion chamber, the spark generated by the spark plug is hot enough to initiate combustion, although it still won't be as complete as it would be in an engine running at optimum temperature.

The final major component of an internal combustion engine is the **lubrication system**. Both gasoline engines (except for most outboards) and diesels rely upon a pool of lubricating oil located in the bottom of the block or **crankcase**. This oil, which is either pumped to or splashed on all critical engine components, usually is circulated through a **filter** to keep it clean.

While the principal job of oil in a gasoline engine is reducing friction, it also takes away heat from some critical components and dumps it into the main supply of oil where it dissipates, mainly by radiation.

The effectiveness of oil is directly related to its ability to flow, or its **viscosity**, which in turn is largely controlled by its temperature. Oil of the improper viscosity will be too thick to flow into small passages when it's cold or too thin to form a protective film when it's hot. In both cases the result is metal touching metal and vastly accelerated wear. Choosing oil of the proper viscosity, keeping it clean, and ensuring it gets neither too hot nor too cold are crucial to a gasoline stern drive engine.

We've just discussed the basic components of the internal combustion engine. Next, we'll look at how stern drive and outboard gasoline engines differ. We'll see how a gasoline-powered engine that uses the four-stroke cycle differs from one using the two-stroke cycle. For our purposes, we'll assume all gasoline-powered stern drives use the four-stroke cycle while all outboards use the two-stroke cycle.

How the Four-Cycle Gasoline Engine Works

As the name implies, the **four-stroke cycle** (or as it's commonly called, the four-cycle) gasoline engine requires that each piston make four strokes—two up and two down—to generate one stroke of power. While there are wide variations among four-stroke gasoline engines, all follow the basic operating principles outlined below.

Virtually all four-cycle marine gasoline engines have two **valves** in the cylinder head for every cylinder. One opens to admit a charge of fuel and air, the other to allow exhaust gases to escape from the combustion chamber. Each valve is activated by an **eccentric** (an egg-shaped lobe) on a **camshaft** that is gear-driven off the crankshaft. The high spot on the turning camshaft raises a **push rod** and activates a lever, or **rocker arm**, that depresses and opens the valve. A spring on each valve closes the valve firmly when the eccentric passes. This system ensures that each valve opens and closes at precisely the same point during the piston's trip up and down the cylinder.

The four-stroke cycle begins with the piston at the top and headed down the cylinder, and with both valves closed. Thanks to the seal created by the piston rings, the piston creates negative pressure within the combustion chamber as it moves downward. When the **intake valve** opens early in the piston's downward journey (the **exhaust valve** remains closed), the charge of fuel and air rushes in and continues to do so until the piston is roughly at the bottom of its travel. When it reaches this point, the first or **intake stroke** is completed.

Somewhere near the bottom of the piston's travel the intake valve closes, sealing the chamber. As the piston moves up the cylinder, it compresses the fuel/air mixture to somewhere around one-ninth its original volume. Thus is completed the second or **compression stroke**.

6

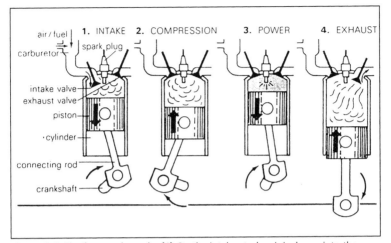

Figure 2-1 The four-stroke cycle. **(1)** On the intake stroke air is drawn into the cylinder as the piston descends. **(2)** During the compression stroke, valves close off the chamber and the piston rises, compressing and heating the air. **(3)** In the power stroke the spark plug ignites the air and fuel mixture; the explosion forces the piston down the cylinder. **(4)** The piston rises again during the exhaust stroke, pushing air out the exhaust valve.

When the piston is at the top of its travel (actually slightly before) the spark plug fires, igniting the mixture and causing it to expand rapidly, driving the piston down the cylinder, turning the crankshaft, and eventually, the propeller. Once the piston is near the bottom of the cylinder and the hot gases have cooled so there is little expansion left, this expansion or **power stroke** is complete. But the cycle isn't over yet.

With the piston now roughly at the bottom of the cylinder, the combustion chamber is full of burned gases that are almost totally lacking in oxygen. Before another power stroke can take place, these gases must be evacuated from the cylinder. To do that, the exhaust valve opens and the piston moves up the cylinder, forcing most of the gases out through the open exhaust valve and into the atmosphere. Once the piston is about at the top of its travel, this fourth or **exhaust stroke** is complete and the cylinder is ready for another charge of fresh air and a new operating cycle.

As you can see, throughout a **power cycle** an engine acts as an air pump. This action explains why the four-cycle gasoline engine is more fuel-efficient than the two-cycle outboard. The two strokes missing in the outboard are those devoted solely to pulling fuel and air into the cylinder and pumping exhaust gases out. Because the two-cycle engine combines these strokes with the other two, it is less efficient at getting a new, fresh charge into each cylinder and removing the spent gases, a process engineers call **scavenging**. On the other hand, every other stroke generated by the two-cycle gasoline engine is a power stroke, so this type of engine typically produces more horsepower than a four-cycle engine of the same size.

The Fuel System

One reason the four-cycle stern drive power system has been so popular over the years is its similarity to an automotive engine. The engine in your boat is identical to that in your car to a large degree, but there are significant differences. One is the fuel system. To meet stringent air-pollution control regulations the automobile's fuel system must be able to make constant, minute adjustments in the fuel-to-air ratio load, temperature, and even atmospheric pressure change. That requires a sophisticated fuel-injection system controlled by a microcomputer that draws engine operating data from a network of sensors.

Someday such regulations may extend to pleasure boats; then the stern drive's gasoline engine will be equipped with a similar fuel system. For now, however, virtually all stern drive engines rely on that simplest, cheapest, and most time-proven device, the **carburetor**, to properly mix fuel and air into a volatile, easily ignitable mixture. Here's how this fuel system works.

The Fuel Pump

Fuel is pulled from the fuel tank by a mechanical **fuel pump**, which on most V engines is located on the lower right front side of the block. There is often also a **fuel filter**, which usually looks like a spin-on oil filter. It is usually located upstream of the fuel pump.

Fuel usually comes to the pump through a synthetic rubber **fuel line** that allows the engine to vibrate without stressing or breaking the line. The outlet line from the pump going to the carburetor is metal, however, to minimize the chance of leakage. Unlike diesel fuel, gasoline is highly volatile and its fumes are highly explosive, so it is critical to avoid even the chance of leakage. Keep this in mind whenever you or anyone works on your engine's fuel system.

The fuel pump is powered by a lever that moves up and down as it tracks an eccentric driven off the crankshaft inside the engine. Consequently, the faster the engine turns, the more fuel it pumps.

Up to this point, the fuel pump on your boat engine is identical to that on your car, so much so that if your boat and car had the same engine model their fuel pumps theoretically could be swapped. The marine model, however, has one small but critical feature. Look at the lower half of a marine fuel pump and you will see a plastic tube (usually bright yellow) running from it to the carburetor. In your car, when the fuel pump fails, it alerts you by leaking gasoline on the floor or pavement—a messy but not particularly dangerous situation because there is almost always sufficient air circulation to dissipate the explosive vapors.

Without the yellow tube, if the fuel pump on your stern drive were to fail, it would most likely leak gasoline into the bilge. The fuel and its fumes would collect until there was a concentration sufficient for an explosion, which could be triggered by virtually any spark, even that from a bilge pump. Instead a marine fuel pump is designed with a sealed lower unit where leaking fuel collects. When the bowl is full the plastic tube carries the fuel up to the carburetor. This floods the engine, causing a misfire or outright stoppage, alerting you to the problem.

If your stern drive engine needs a new fuel pump you could save a few dollars by purchasing an automotive unit without the sealed lower unit and plastic overflow tube. But you would be courting disaster should the automotive replacement pump fail. Don't use anything but a Coast Guard–approved marine fuel pump.

The Flame Arrestor

The other half of the four-cycle gasoline marine fuel system is the carburetor. Before we examine the marine carburetor, let's look at the item on top of it.

Either in clear view or sitting beneath a protective "rain hat" you'll find a silver- or copper-colored metal cap with slots or openings around its sides to admit air. It looks something like an air filter. While it can prevent larger debris from entering the carburetor, most engine builders feel the marine environment is sufficiently dust-free to preclude the need for the automotive-style air cleaner. This device serves a different purpose.

It's a **flame arrestor** and, like the yellow tube leading from fuel pump to carburetor, it is a safety element designed specifically for the marine environment. If the engine's ignition timing is sufficiently mal-

Figure 3-1 An emergency line runs from the fuel pump to the carburetor.

adjusted or its cylinders become saturated with fuel during a prolonged effort to start the engine, ignition can occur while the intake valve is still open. The explosion can travel back through the intake system and out the carburetor opening.

This untimely ignition in an automobile is less damaging because the engine is surrounded by plenty of air. When this happens in a boat's engine, which is in the bilge where there's relatively little air movement, the result could be an engine fire or worse. The flame arrestor prevents a **backfire** from leaving the carburetor; it always should be in place when the engine is being cranked or is running.

In spite of what you may have heard, removing the flame arrestor will not improve performance; the unit simply doesn't offer enough resistance to incoming air to make any noticeable difference. Taking it off will only place you, your passengers, and your boat at risk.

The Carburetor

Whether on a boat, a car, or a lawn mower motor, a carburetor has two basic jobs: to effectively mix gasoline and air into an atomized, vaporous, easily ignitable mixture with the correct proportions of each; and to adjust the amount of fuel-to-air mixture admitted to the cylinders to control engine speed and power. It also must modify the fuel-to-air ratio (or mixture) by adding more fuel (enriching the mixture) to provide easier cold starts.

The mixture of fuel and air in just the right proportion takes place in the **venturi** or barrel. Carburetors may have one, two, or four venturis, depending on the size and power of the engine they serve. The venturi is nothing more than a carefully sized restriction in the carburetor through which air being sucked into the engine must pass. As the air passes through this restriction its velocity increases, lowering the ambient pressure in the venturi.

A machined passage or **jet**, also of a specific size, leads from a small fuel reservoir, the **carburetor bowl**, in the carburetor into the venturi. The low pressure there sucks an exact amount of gasoline through the tube and into the venturi where it hits the high-speed air and is dispersed into a vapor. The greater the speed of the air moving through the venturi, the more fuel is drawn from the carburetor bowl. Adjustable **needle valves** can modify the amount of fuel that passes through each jet, thereby changing the ratio of fuel to air. A simple **float valve** in the carburetor bowl keeps it full of fuel. Some carburetors have two bowls, one in front and one in back.

The volume of air that passes through the venturi controls the volume of fuel; together they control the power output of the engine. What controls the volume of air is a simple flapper or **butterfly valve** in the intake air passage downstream of the venturi. When you put your foot on the accelerator in your car or push the throttle lever forward in your boat, you twist this butterfly valve open, allowing more air (and therefore more fuel) to enter the engine. When you reduce speed, the valve closes, restricting both air and fuel, and reducing power.

The Choke

When an engine is cold, combustion requires a higher proportion of gasoline in the charge than when it's warm. To effect this, a second flapper valve called the **choke plate** is located upstream of the venturi

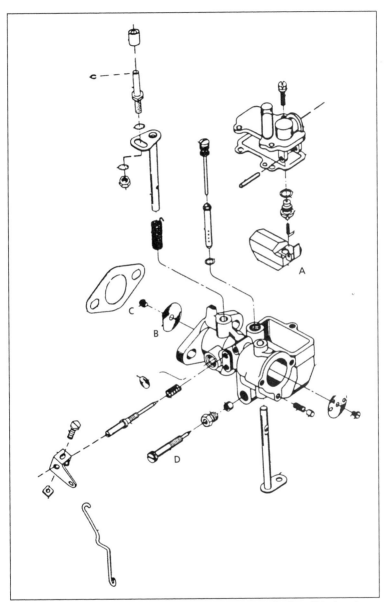

Figure 3-2 An exploded view of a typical carburetor. Note the float **(A)**, throttle plate **(B)**, choke plate **(C)**, and the adjustable mixture screw **(D)**. This is a sidedraft carburetor used on an outboard. Most stern drives use downdraft carbs, which are mechanically almost identical.(Courtesy OMC)

and is usually controlled by a spring that is warmed by either a small electrical current or the heat of the engine. When the engine is cold the spring retracts, closing the choke plate and restricting air flow. Because the choke plate is upstream of the venturi, it alters the otherwise constant ratio of fuel to air, enriching the mixture and making it more combustible. As the engine (and spring) warms, the spring expands, opening the choke plate until the flow of air entering the venturi is unrestricted.

The Accelerator Pump

There is one more component in our simple carburetor worth discussing. Because the flow of fuel takes a moment to adjust to the increased flow of air when the throttle is opened suddenly, there can be an annoying lag between throttle movement and engine reaction. To avoid this, the carburetor usually has a device called an **accelerator pump** that pulls a shot of gasoline from the carburetor bowl and injects it directly into the venturi when the throttle opens suddenly. This allows the engine to respond more quickly.

Because this system is purely mechanical and not dependent on air flow through the venturi, it occurs even when the engine isn't running. That means that, with the engine off, you can remove the flame arrestor, look down into the carburetor, open the throttle linkage fully, and see the gasoline spurt right into the venturi. This is often the fastest way to determine whether gasoline is getting to the carburetor—a big help in troubleshooting an engine that won't run.

Air flows through the carburetor due to a partial vacuum inside the cylinders caused by the descending pistons. As we'll see, once the intake valve opens, this vacuum pulls air through the flame arrestor, the venturi, and the passages of the **intake manifold** into the cylinder where combustion can occur.

The Ignition System

If the four-cycle gasoline engine has a weak link it is the ignition system. The reason is simple: High voltage and a damp environment don't mix. Add a little salt, which increases both the rate of corrosion and the conductivity of water, and you have the potential for serious problems. If you have an engine problem, chances are it is in the electrical/ignition system. For all these reasons, it's important to understand how your stern drive's ignition system works and how to take care of it.

Fortunately ignition system maintenance is as simple as ignition system design. In keeping with the philosophy of this book, our basic explanation will not get involved with electrical theory.

Like so much of this engine, the four-cycle's ignition system is nearly identical to that found in most late-model automobiles. It has two primary functions. One is to boost **12-volt battery** or **alternator current** to between 20,000 and 40,000 volts, so it can jump the 0.035-inch air gap between a spark plug's **electrodes**. The other is to make sure the spark plug fires at precisely the right time.

The basic mechanism for boosting voltage is the **ignition coil**, usually a black cylinder with two small wires that carry 12-volt current to it and one large wire that carries high-voltage current from it to the **distributor**.

The Distributor

The distributor's job is to get this high-voltage charge to the right spark plug at the right time. It's recognizable by the many heavy wires coming out of its **cap**. The center wire connects to the coil, while each of those around the perimeter leads to a single spark plug.

Inside the distributor is a vertical shaft that turns at the same speed as the engine. Atop this shaft and inside the distributor cap is the **rotor**, a contact in its center, and another at its long end. The center one constantly touches a contact in the cap that receives current from the coil wire. As it turns, the end contact touches each of the contacts in the cap that are connected to the spark plug wires. Since the rotor spins at engine speed, it touches each contact once every engine revolution. All these contacts wear, and eventually will cease to carry enough current to fire the plug.

The order in which the cylinders fire theoretically is determined by the order of the spark plug wires on the cap; in reality, an engine only will run properly with a specific firing order.

The process by which the coil increases voltage from 12 volts to 20,000 volts requires a switch that can momentarily stop the supply of voltage to the coil just before the spark plug fires. In many stern drive engines, this switch is a pair of **breaker points** (or simply "points") inside the distributor. These hinged contacts ride on a portion of the distributor shaft that is fitted with high spots or **lobes**, so the set closes (makes contact) and opens (breaks contact) at precisely the right time. The spacing between points is referred to as **dwell**. If the points do not open just the right amount, either they will close at the wrong time or a spark will jump across them, preventing voltage build-up and burning the points' surface.

The **condenser**, which is also inside the distributor cap, absorbs excessive voltage from the coil so the current doesn't jump the gap between the open points and so prevent the voltage from increasing. The condenser usually is replaced at the same time as the points.

Because points require periodic adjustment and replacement, many newer engines have done away with them. Instead of moving parts, such systems use electrical impulses to open and close the circuit. The principal advantage of this **electronic ignition system** is that it's essentially maintenance-free. The disadvantage is that when it goes bad the engine quits—usually without warning—and the only way to fix it is to replace the entire electronic module at an expense well above that of a set of points. In some designs the engine can still "limp home" even if the electronic module fails; in others the engine simply stops dead.

Exactly when the spark plugs fire is called **ignition timing**. In most systems it's regulated by loosening a bolt and turning the distributor one way to make the spark plugs fire sooner (advancing the timing) or turning it the other to make them fire later (retarding the timing). At slow speeds the spark plugs fire just before the piston reaches the top of the cylinder, so that by the time the fuel actually burns, the piston is in position to be forced down. As engine speed increases the piston moves faster, but the time necessary for the fuel to ignite remains the same. To compensate the spark plug must fire a little earlier to "lead" the piston. This is called **ignition advance**. The ignition system may use a mechanical or vacuum advance system, or a combination of both. Electronic ignition systems may advance the timing electronically. Fortunately advance systems rarely need adjustment or service, unless the small vacuum hose leading to the distributor leaks or becomes disconnected. If the advance system fails, the engine typically will run fine at slow speeds but misfire or backfire as the throttle is opened.

As you can imagine, wires leading from the distributor to the spark plug must be well insulated. If they weren't, the 20,000-volt current would jump to some other component such as the engine block, which is "ground" in this electrical circuit, and the spark plug would fail to fire.

Although spark plug wires can wear out after many hours, the most likely source of trouble is where the wire connects to the spark plug. Here the contact may loosen from being pulled off and pushed on too many times, or its protective rubber boot may become brittle and cracked, allowing moisture or oil to enter. Under these circumstances the current will short circuit to ground and the spark plug will misfire.

Spark Plugs

Spark plugs are relatively simply devices designed to make sure that high-voltage current stays isolated from the surrounding cylinder head so a strong spark will jump the gap between spark plug tip and spark plug electrode.

There are three things to remember about spark plugs. First, choose the right one. A spark plug must fit into the hole in the cylinder head, but it must also have the proper heat range, a measure of its ability to dissipate heat produced by combustion. A spark plug that gets too hot wears out quickly; one too cold becomes fouled by unburned fuel and fails to fire. Choose the spark plug recommended by your engine builder and you should have no problem with heat range unless you operate under unusual conditions.

The second consideration is proper installation. Before you install a spark plug you must adjust the gap between the tip and electrode. Spark plugs are not properly gapped when you buy them. For this job you'll need the recommended spark plug gap from your manual and an inexpensive **feeler gauge** with a small notched tool to bend the electrode. The electrode shouldn't need much force. Use a light touch and you won't get the electrode out of alignment with the tip.

The spark plug also must be tightened enough to prevent leaks, yet not be so tight that it's damaged. Most mechanics can feel when

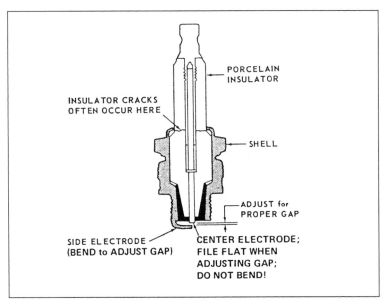

PORCELAIN
INSULATOR

INSULATOR CRACKS
OFTEN OCCUR HERE

SHELL

ADJUST for
PROPER GAP

SIDE ELECTRODE
(BEND to ADJUST GAP)

CENTER ELECTRODE;
FILE FLAT WHEN
ADJUSTING GAP;
DO NOT BEND!

Figure 4-1 A cutaway view of a typical spark plug. (Courtesy Mercury Marine)

they've cranked a plug down hard enough to collapse its brass gasket and get a good seal without causing damage. If you haven't developed such a feel, rent a **torque wrench**, which will tell you exactly how tight you're twisting the plugs. You should find spark plug torque specifications in your owner's manual, but if you can't locate them, 14 pound-feet is usually a safe number.

Finally maintain your plugs. Thanks to unleaded gasoline, spark plugs enjoy a long life today. Although many boat owners prefer to replace plugs each year, most plugs should last at least 300 hours before replacement. For most people this works out to two to three boating seasons. However, there is no arguing that a fresh set of plugs every spring is cheap insurance.

Above all, remember this about the ignition system: It is designed to provide a spark of sufficient strength to jump an air gap of 0.035 inch. This ability not only ensures your engine will run efficiently, it also means the current can jump other gaps. High-voltage current will always take the path of least resistance, which might be a hairline crack in your distributor cap or spark plug insulator, a dirty spark plug boot, or even a piece of frayed or worn spark plug wire.

Keep all the high-voltage components of your engine clean and in proper condition and you'll vastly reduce the chances of ignition problems. And that means fewer engine problems overall.

The Cooling System

Regardless of the number of strokes in its power cycle or where it is installed, the internal combustion engine is designed first to produce heat, then to put it to work. But the amount of heat must be restricted to a relatively narrow range. Too little heat means the engine is inefficient and makes too little power. Too much heat means damage to or even destruction of the engine. It is the job of the cooling system to ensure that an engine strikes just the right balance between the two extremes.

The basic principle of most engine cooling systems is **heat exchange**; that is, transferring excess heat of combustion to some other medium and away from the engine. In your car, heat exchange is effected by a recirculating supply of **coolant** that pulls heat from the block around which it circulates. The coolant then travels to the radiator where it transfers this heat through the walls of the radiator and into the surrounding air that passes over it. Not surprisingly, the automotive radiator is technically termed a water-to-air heat exchanger.

Instead of transferring engine heat to air, a boat's cooling system transfers it to the virtually unlimited supply of relatively cool water in which the boat floats. It can do this one of two ways: through a raw-water cooling system or a fresh-water cooling system.

Raw-Water Cooling

A raw-water cooling system uses an engine-driven **water pump** to pull water into the boat through **intake holes**, circulate it through all internal cavities, and then pump it back out. In some stern drives this pump is mounted on the front of the engine; in others it is hidden from view, inside the drive unit. Some of the cooling water may pass from

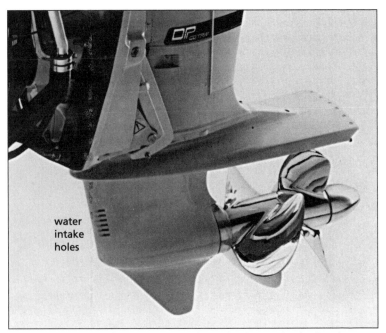

water
intake
holes

Figure 5-1 This view of a stern drive unit shows the six water intake slots that are on each side of the unit. Some stern drives have separate water pickups. (Courtesy Volvo)

the block into the **exhaust elbow** where, as we'll see in the next chapter, it helps cool and quiet the exhaust. The rest may exit through a bypass at the transom, through a passage in the drive unit, or both. Regardless of its route, the coolant is warmer when it leaves the engine than when it enters. Therefore, the engine is cooler.

The main advantages of a raw-water cooling system are simplicity and low cost. Other than the raw-water pump, the only other components are the circulating pump on the front of the engine (the same to which, in automotive applications, the fan mounts); a **thermostat**, which restricts coolant flow to speed warm-up and to help the engine maintain a minimum temperature; and a few hoses, usually leading from the engine **coolant jacket** to the **exhaust manifold**.

The practicality of a raw-water cooling system is dependent on the quality of the water. Such systems can offer years of trouble-free service in fresh-water lakes and rivers. But in polluted and salt water, the result can be corrosion and the build-up of scale and deposits in internal passages. This scale inhibits the transfer of heat and can restrict the passage of cooling water, eventually causing overheating.

Fresh-Water Cooling

The alternative to the raw-water cooling system is the fresh-water cooling system in which heat transfer takes place between two separate streams of coolant. One is a closed loop that is circulated via the engine pump through all internal passages. Its last stop is a water-to-water heat exchanger—basically a radiator surrounded by water instead of air. The raw water, propelled by a separate raw-water pump, passes over this heat exchanger taking away heat. The coolant in the closed loop is typically the same type used in your automobile, meaning it's formulated to resist corrosion. Its circulation is controlled by a thermostat.

The advantage of the fresh-water cooling system is that it virtually eliminates corrosion within the closed loop as long as you maintain the concentration and effectiveness of the coolant. Corrosion still can occur within the raw-water loop, including in the exhaust elbows and the heat exchanger itself. The heat exchanger is typically brass, which is naturally resistant to corrosion. It is also protected by **zinc pencils**, or anodes. Because the only purpose of these zincs is to corrode before other metal parts, they are often called sacrificial zincs. Their corroding does not affect the integrity of the system and they are easy and cheap to replace. However, once these zincs completely dissolve, other more expensive and critical parts of the system will begin to corrode.

The fresh-water cooling system also does a better job of maintaining a steady, optimum operating temperature than does the raw-water system. That's important because the colder an engine runs, the lower its efficiency. A less efficient engine not only burns more fuel, it also forms more combustion deposits and gets less effective lubrication because its oil doesn't get as warm and so doesn't flow as freely. However, the differences in efficiency and lubrication aren't of sufficient magnitude for the average boater to ever notice. Indeed, many commercial fishing boats are powered by raw-water cooled gasoline engines.

The Exhaust System

Like the exhaust system in your automobile, the one in your boat is designed to route hot toxic exhaust gases safely out of the engine and into the atmosphere, directing them in such a way that they won't be inhaled by passengers. Both systems also incorporate **silencers** to reduce the sound produced by combustion, although boats silence exhaust differently than do cars and trucks.

To this list of jobs that must be performed by the exhaust system, a boat adds yet another: to keep temperatures in the engine compartment low enough to avoid the danger of fire or burns. This isn't necessary with cars or trucks because their design allows plenty of fresh air to circulate as the vehicle moves, which keeps temperatures within acceptable limits. By contrast, a stern drive engine is mounted deep in the bilge. The air that circulates here is not nearly enough to offset the heat produced by the typical exhaust system. Moreover, heat reduces the density of air in the engine compartment, which can rob an engine of power.

Since the engine block is encapsulated in a water jacket, radiated heat is not a significant problem. The problem is heat radiated by exhaust after it leaves the engine, specifically at the exhaust manifold and exhaust pipe.

For the exhaust manifolds, the solution is the same as that used with the engine block: Encapsulate them in a jacket of water, which not only reduces heat radiation but also removes some of the heat from the exhaust gases. As exhaust gases cool, they lose much of their acoustic energy. To further reduce heat and damp noise as well, water is injected into the exhaust stream.

Stern drives are designed with an inverted **U** on top and just down-

Figure 6-1 This cutaway of a Yamaha exhaust riser, elbow, and manifold shows the water and exhaust passages.

stream of the exhaust manifold. This **U** prevents water from flowing back into the engine even if the boat is put into reverse. Raw water is injected into this exhaust elbow just after its highest point, reducing the temperature of the gases.

Most stern drive engines have exhaust manifolds encased in a water jacket to keep them cool, although the exhaust gases and coolant water are segregated until they reach the exhaust elbow. If water injected into them is relatively clean and not salty, these manifolds may last a long time—perhaps the life of the engine. If the boat operates in salt, brackish, or highly polluted water, manifolds and elbows will corrode and eventually require replacement.

Usually the exhaust elbow is the component most susceptible to corrosion because it is where hot exhaust gases and water mix. Downstream of here the exhaust is cooler and diluted, and therefore less corrosive.

In most stern drives, exhaust gases and water leave the exhaust elbow, pass through a hose that goes through the transom and into the internal passage in the drive unit, and finally exit underwater through the propeller or through a bypass opening. However when the boat is at rest or barely moving, the force necessary to push the exhaust through the propeller and against the water produces enough back pressure to inhibit engine performance, and even to burn exhaust valves. To overcome this, stern drives have an **exhaust bypass circuit**

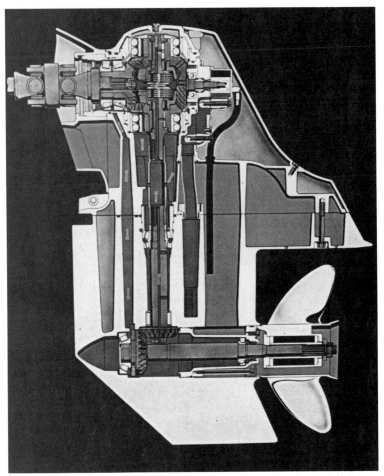

Figure 6-2 Cutaway illustration of the internal exhaust passages in a typical drive unit. (Courtesy OMC)

in the unit that allows the exhaust to exit at the transom. This causes the bubbling you may hear and see in your boat at idle. As the boat speeds up, more gases can flow freely through the propeller because of the water flowing past it.

The process of injecting water into the exhaust to cool it and making the water exit underwater through the propeller alleviates the need for a muffler in a stern drive. On the other hand, it requires an exhaust system complicated by hoses and water jackets and periodic maintenance of exhaust parts subject to corrosion.

The Lubrication System

The object of the internal combustion engine is the production of power that can do work. Its primary ally is the heat generated by combustion, which forces the piston down. Its greatest enemy is friction, which constantly resists all movement, reduces efficiency, and causes wear. The modern internal combustion engine employs many weapons to reduce friction—weapons such as high-tech bearings and supersmooth operating surfaces. But the biggest weapon of all is the same one engineers have relied upon since they first fired up an engine: lubrication.

Lubrication is basically simple. Even the most highly machined surface is covered with microscopic irregularities that cause friction. Think of them as tiny ridges and peaks. When two such surfaces rub against each other they create resistance, which produces heat and wear. Oil reduces this resistance by forming a film between the surfaces that keeps them from touching. Because it is a circulating liquid, oil also removes heat that can cause damage. Because it naturally displaces moisture, lubricating oil also prevents rust and slows oxidation.

To basic refined crude oil petroleum engineers add a number of chemicals and compounds, each of which performs a specific job such as improving slipperiness, making oil flow more easily when it's cold, allowing it to keep dirt particles suspended until they can be removed by a filter or until the oil is drained, and helping to neutralize harmful acids that can eat away soft bearing surfaces. Together these chemicals form the **additive package**.

The refining and production of high-quality lubricating oil is an immensely complicated process. The process by which an engine uses those oils to prevent wear and damage is simple. The lubrication systems of all four-cycle gasoline engines have three main components. One is a **reservoir** of sufficient capacity to allow some oil to be constantly circulated while the rest sits and cools. In the four-cycle engine, this reservoir is formed by a pan that bolts to the bottom of the engine block. Most gasoline-powered stern drive engines hold between four and five quarts in their oil pans when they're not running.

The second component is the **oil pump**, usually contained inside the oil pan. It is gear-driven off the crankshaft, so that the faster the engine turns the more oil is pumped. An oil pump is a simple device, actually nothing more than a pair of counter-rotating gears. As these gears turn they force oil through a series of drilled passages in the block and crankshaft, so that every critical component is fed a constant stream of fresh oil. (Some components, especially parts of the crankshaft, are lubricated simply by oil being constantly splashed on them.) Oil is typically pumped to the highest point of the engine (usually the rocker arms in the valve train), then drains back into the oil pan by gravity.

The third important component of the lubrication system is the **oil filter**. Again a simple device, it's typically a canister of treated paper, which traps small particles of dirt and metal shavings as the oil is forced through it by the oil pump. Since the filter is paper-based it also absorbs some moisture, an important benefit since moisture reduces oil's effectiveness and produces gum and harmful deposits.

Most engines incorporate a **bypass valve** at the oil filter so that if the filter becomes clogged the oil can go around the filter and on to the rest of the engine. This means that even with a clogged filter parts still get lubricated, although with contaminated, unfiltered oil.

The Stern Drive Propulsion System

Although basic design varies, all major stern drive propulsion systems perform certain duties. All attach to the engine's crankshaft and pass power from it through two 90-degree **gear sets**. Thus, power produced by an engine inside a boat can turn a propeller that is outside the hull and a couple of feet below it. The gear sets allow a boat to use a four-cycle automotive-style engine, which is more efficient than a lighter two-cycle outboard hanging on the transom. Moreover this setup permits engine placement deep in the bilge and under the deck, well protected from the harsh marine environment.

Inboard drive systems use unarticulated automotive-based four-cycle engines. In other words, the propeller cannot move from side to side or pivot up and down. Because the stern drive's engine is **articulated**, it does not need a separate rudder and steering gear. Articulation provides better maneuverability and steering response since the direction of propeller thrust can change, which means a pilot can change the boat's running attitude to suit water and operating conditions, and tilt the drive enough to beach or trailer it without damaging it.

Like outboards, stern drives contain internal mechanisms for changing the direction of propeller rotation. These mechanisms operate similar to a car's transmission, offering forward, reverse, or neutral. They also eliminate the need for a separate, external transmission, reducing the size of the system while increasing the boat's flexibility and maneuverability.

What follows is a basic explanation of how the stern drive works. There are many variations on this basic theme, but the principles and

operational procedures are largely identical. And that's what you need
to know.

The Path of Power

A stern drive consists of five main parts: the **gimbal housing**, which
bolts to the outside of the transom; the **transom plate**, which bolts to
the inside, and the exterior **upper, intermediate, and lower units**.
Power passes from the engine through a hole in the transom and into
the upper unit. The shaft carrying power from the engine connects to a
universal joint, which allows power to be transmitted without binding
the upper unit while it moves from side to side and up and down. A
simple tiller connected to the upper unit gives you the ability to steer.
The tiller's movement may or may not be power-assisted by the same
kind of belt-driven **hydraulic pump** you probably have on your car.
Trimming and tilting are done by **hydraulic cylinders** on either side of
the drive. These cylinders attach to the **transom shield** at one end and
the intermediate unit at the other. The pump for these cylinders is
electrically operated.

The complete stern drive unit hangs on the exterior of the boat and

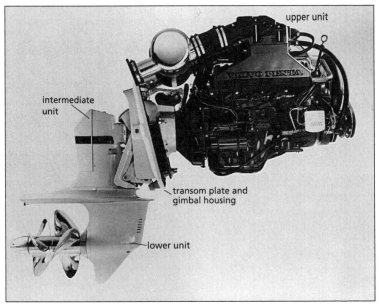

Figure 8-1 The five basic components of the stern drive propulsion system are the
upper, intermediate, and lower units, the gimbal housing and the transom plate.
Note the two counter-rotating propellers on this Volvo Penta.

is carried on a gimbal that attaches to the transom shield and allows the drive unit fully articulated movement. The transom shield bolts through the transom and through the transom plate inside the boat. This plate also carries the weight of the after part of the engine. The movable engine mounts bolt to the boat's stringers and carry the forward weight.

On most stern drive units, the shaft that attaches to the drive unit side of the universal joint terminates in a **pinion gear** that meshes with another pinion gear and shaft that is roughly vertical. Builders can match different pinions with different numbers of teeth to alter the final **gear ratio** of the drive unit.

The vertical shaft leaves this pinion set and passes through the intermediate unit, terminating in the lower unit. On most units about midway down this shaft is a toothed portion that drives the raw-water pump. The shaft terminates at another pinion gear that allows another 90-degree change of direction so that the output shaft is roughly horizontal and parallel to the engine's crankshaft.

At this point, the shaft is permanently engaged with the engine, so some sort of mechanism is necessary to disengage it and shift it from forward to reverse. The solution is the same mechanism used in most outboards: the **dog clutch**. Indeed, the lower unit of most stern drives is virtually identical to that of an outboard of similar horsepower.

The pinion gear at which the vertical shaft terminates constantly meshes with two horizontal pinion gears, one forward and the other to the rear. This placement means that one gear constantly turns clockwise while the other constantly turns counter-clockwise.

The Dog Clutch

On the inside face of each of these horizontal pinions is a **dog**, basically a circular piece of metal with square protrusions and matching indentations, so that the dog looks like the top wall of a castle. Between these two counter-rotating gear-dog sets is a **double-dog piece**, with an identical castellated surface facing each of the counter-rotating dogs. This piece is designed to slide horizontally along the propeller shaft, always turning with it.

When the double-dog set is exactly in the middle, it engages neither the front nor rear dog, thus providing neutral. When you move the **throttle/shift lever** in one direction, the double-dog set slides forward, clunks into place, and the propeller turns in one direction. When the throttle/control is moved in the opposite direction, the center dog set moves out of engagement with the forward dog, through the middle where there is no engagement, and clunks into engagement with the rear dog, providing the opposite propeller rotation.

As you can see, the main advantage of the dog clutch is its durabil-

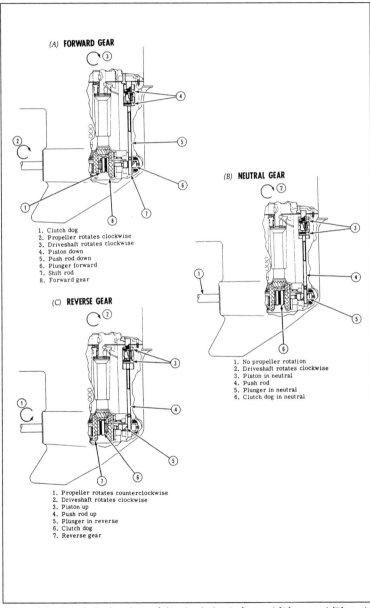

(A) **FORWARD GEAR**

1. Clutch dog
2. Propeller rotates clockwise
3. Driveshaft rotates clockwise
4. Piston down
5. Push rod down
6. Plunger forward
7. Shift rod
8. Forward gear

(B) **NEUTRAL GEAR**

1. No propeller rotation
2. Driveshaft rotates clockwise
3. Piston in neutral
4. Push rod
5. Plunger in neutral
6. Clutch dog in neutral

(C) **REVERSE GEAR**

1. Propeller rotates counterclockwise
2. Driveshaft rotates clockwise
3. Piston up
4. Push rod up
5. Plunger in reverse
6. Clutch dog
7. Reverse gear

Figure 8-2 The relative locations of the clutch dog in forward **(A)**, neutral **(B)**, and reverse **(C)**. The three holes immediately above are cooling water intakes for the powerhead. (Courtesy OMC)

ity and simplicity. It's been proven in decades of use and it has relatively few moving parts. Its principal disadvantages are the clunk when the dogs engage and the limits on the amount of **torque** (or twisting force) it can handle.

The sides of the dogs incline slightly. These "ramps" allow the dogs to engage and disengage more easily, but they also mean that if sufficient twisting force is applied, the dogs can pop out of engagement on their own. Typically, it takes a large, powerful engine to make this happen, usually a 7.4-liter or larger V-8. In engines of smaller displacement, accidental disengagement is rare.

The dog clutch has a third, relatively minor disadvantage. It's difficult and expensive to set up two identical dog-clutch stern drives so that one propeller turns one way and the other turns the opposite. Many boat owners prefer "counter-rotating propellers" because they feel this setup makes the boat track straighter. Unfortunately dog-clutch stern drives can turn in opposite directions only when one unit is built differently, and that means more expense.

The Cone Clutch

The **cone clutch** is an alternative that addresses these disadvantages. Its shifting is smooth, its torque-carrying capacity is limited only by the strength of its components, and it provides counter-rotation by

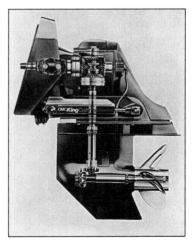

Figure 8-3 An alternative to the dog clutch is the cone clutch, an exploded view of which is shown at left. (Courtesy OMC)

simply changing the position of an easy-to-reach lever. At present, all Volvo Pentas, MerCruiser Bravos, and OMC King Cobras use the cone clutch.

In the cone-clutch drive, the clutch is in the upper unit and the lower unit houses only the two pinion gears used to change the final drive ratio. Instead of dogs, the cone clutch depends upon a **screw-type engagement**, which means the greater the force applied, the stronger the engagement. The screw design also permits a more gradual engagement and eliminates the clunk. The design is such that rotation can be changed by simply shifting the position of the link at the clutch from one side to the other, which changes the direction in which the cone slides.

Is the cone clutch better than the dog clutch? The answer depends upon personal preference, specifically whether the clunk of engagement bothers you and whether you need counter-rotation. As far as torque-handling capacity, as long as you don't significantly modify the engine that came with your drive, you shouldn't have to worry about a dog clutch slipping out of gear.

Trim and Tilt

Because it can move forward and back along the axis of the keel, the stern drive allows a boater to adjust the angle of thrust inward, which keeps the bow down and allows the boat to plane faster while maintaining better visibility. Once the boat is on plane, the boater can raise the bow to reduce the amount of hull touching the water, thereby improving performance and efficiency. If the boater extends the drive even farther out, the boat can be operated in shallow water or put on a trailer or a beach without dragging.

The way the stern drive does this is simple. On either side of the intermediate unit are **hydraulic trim cylinders**, activated by an electrical pump mounted in the engine compartment. When the operator pushes a button on the control or instrument panel, these cylinders are activated in either direction, depending on which way the boater pushes the button. To activate the **tilt** mode and swing the drive all the way up, the boater may have to hold the button down longer or push another button altogether.

Another feature of this **trim system** is a **kick-up** feature. In most stern drives, there is a **bypass valve** in the cylinders that allows the drive to swing up almost instantly when it hits an object, preventing damage to the lower unit. (Some Volvo Pentas do this mechanically.) The thrust of the propeller eventually forces the drive back into position.

When you look at the typical stern drive unit, you can see that it has space for a lot of things other than the drive shaft, gears, and clutches. Indeed, the unit also contains passages for cooling water to be supplied to the engine and then exhausted back into the water, and passages for exhaust to pass through the unit and out through the propeller. Moreover, gear sets typically run in a special oil that must be periodically changed, so **reservoirs** for it must be included. Obviously it's imperative that the unit segregate the lube oil, raw water, and exhaust; this is done with gaskets and seals.

There is also some variation in the design of the raw-water pumps on the major drive units. Units like the MerCruiser Alpha and Yamaha that are outboard-based have the pumps inside the intermediate unit as described above. To service the pump you detach the lower unit from the intermediate unit by unscrewing a series of bolts. The OMC Cobra raw-water pump is in the rear of the upper unit and is driven off the pinion gear. You access it by removing a plastic cover on the top rear of the unit. Volvo Penta uses a water pump driven off the engine, either from the crankshaft pulley or by a V-belt. Since it's right on the engine, it's usually accessible for servicing.

Two more components worth mentioning that are found on all stern drives are the **anti-cavitation plate** (sometimes called the anti-ventilation plate) and the **trim tab**. The anti-cavitation plate is the wide, flat plate just above the propeller. It runs from the front of the drive to the rear. This plate has two functions: to provide lift and help in planing, and to prevent the propeller from sucking air from the surface, or **ventilating**. Ventilating occurs when the drive unit is trimmed out too far, and results in the engine speeding up as the boat slows down. In this case, the remedy is simply to trim the drive unit down far enough to allow the propeller to bite again.

The trim tab is a small fin on the underside of the anti-ventilation plate immediately above the propeller. Its job is to help offset **steering feedback**, or torque produced by the rotating propeller. Without it, the boat's wheel would constantly pull in one direction, which can quickly tire the person at the helm and in extreme cases be dangerous. Once you loosen the bolt that holds the trim tab, you can rotate the tab in

Figure 8-4 The trim tab is located on the underside of the anti-ventilation plate. The tab can pivot to either side. (Courtesy Mercury Marine)

the opposite direction of the torque, as you would a boat rudder. When the tab is properly adjusted, you should be able to take your hands off the wheel momentarily while the boat follows a relatively straight course.

Volvo Penta offers the Duoprop, a drive with two counter-rotating propellers, that it claims greatly reduces, if not eliminates, steering torque. According to Volvo Penta, the drive is more efficient and provides better response to helm input than single-propeller designs.

Anti-Corrosion Measures

Because the stern drive unit is immersed in water much of its life, corrosion can be a problem. To understand how a stern drive corrodes and how you can prevent it, you need to understand how corrosion works. The most threatening kind of corrosion in the marine environment is **electrolysis**, which occurs when two dissimilar metals are placed in water that contains sufficient impurities to allow it to conduct an electrical current. (This is the same principle by which the typical automotive battery works.) Eventually, one metal dissolves, or corrodes.

The stern drive unit is made of cast aluminum alloy—that is, aluminum with small amounts of other metals added to make it strong and easy to work. If you place this alloy into salt, brackish, or polluted water and there is another, less reactive metal (said to be more inert or nobler) in the same water, the aluminum will dissolve.

Stern drives are protected from such corrosion four ways. First, they are cast from the most corrosion-resistant alloys available. Each manufacturer formulates its own unique alloy that it thinks offers the best mix of strength and corrosion resistance. Second, every component that comes into contact with the water is painted with the hardest, most durable paint available, because if the water can't reach the metal, it can't corrode it. Again, each company has its own unique way of preparing, priming, and painting the castings, as well as its own unique paint formula.

Third, the stern drive unit is equipped with a number of exposed, unpainted zincs because zinc is the metal most susceptible to electrolytic corrosion. Like those in the fresh-water cooling system, these inexpensive, easily replaceable sacrificial zincs dissolve first, saving more costly components. Typical zinc locations are inside the lower unit forward of the propeller, on the underside of the transom shield, and on the upper portion of the lower unit. MerCruiser, for example, makes its trim tab out of zinc, so that as it wears away you are warned by the increased steering torque. Because they are never painted (and never should be) and are in clear view (except for the one ahead of the propeller), zincs are easy to spot. Just look for pieces of silver metal.

As one final step in protecting stern drives, builders make sure everything that might be exposed to water is electrically connected or **bonded** to each other. A component not bonded is not protected by the zincs and will begin to corrode.

The MerCathode

In addition to these anti-corrosion measures, MerCruiser markets an electronic device that stops electrolytic corrosion by imparting a tiny blocking current to the water around the drive. Called Mer-Cathode, the device is compatible with other types of drive units and draws little current from the battery.

PART TWO

How to Operate Your Stern Drive

The Log

Although extremely reliable and durable, the stern drive is neither perfect nor immune to wear and tear. If you operate it wisely and care for it properly, however, it can last as long as the hull that carries it.

The key to maintaining a stern drive, or any mechanical device for that matter, is **systematic maintenance**. And the key to systematic maintenance is keeping good records. No one can predict a catastrophic breakdown, but fortunately, most mechanical problems do not just "pop up" out of the blue. An engine or stern drive unit usually gives fair warning that something is wrong well before it quits. Your job is to know these signs, observe them, and take the proper action when you see them. Your single most valuable tool in observing long-term trends is a **log**, a simple written record of what you observe and what you and others do to your stern drive.

In the following two chapters you'll find two checklists. You should refer to the daily checklist every time you take your boat out, no matter how short the trip. The periodic checklist, which is more involved, you should refer to every month. Each time you conduct a checkup, write the results in your log. Your log can be nothing more than a pocket-size spiral binder. Make sure you store it in a watertight container (a resealable sandwich bag is perfect) and keep it on your boat, so you can make or check entries any time you're aboard.

The following is a list of the basic data you should enter into your log. If you organize your log in chronological order you can quickly locate any event according to the time it occurred.

Record of Maintenance and Repairs
Being able to look at a single record and tell what has been main-

tained or repaired on your engine is a valuable asset. A proper record will detail the kind of work done, the date on which the work was done, the engine hour meter reading when it was done, and the cost. This information also will help you perform maintenance when it should be done, instead of when you think of it. A proper log also should provide space for comments—both yours and a mechanic's—perhaps regarding the cause of a specific problem or the likelihood of future problems.

It's important to note that there is only one yardstick by which to measure everything that happens to your stern drive and that's **engine hours**. There are some cases when a simple chronological interval (days or months) might dictate the need for work or maintenance, but it's far more likely that the determining factor will be the number of hours on the engine since the last service. If your boat is not equipped with an hour meter for each engine, either install one or have one installed immediately. The cost shouldn't exceed $50 per engine and the benefit is well worth the price.

Record of Oil and Fuel Consumption

Adding a quart of oil is as forgettable an event as it is important. If you don't write it down, you'll never remember when you last added oil or how much you added. That means you'll have no idea how

Maintenance and Repair Log				
Date	**Work done**	**Engine hours**	**Cost**	**Remarks**
9/10/89	—	4280-91	—	passage St. Lucie to Miami
9/12/89	spark plug change	4294	$62.30	Steven's Marine
9/21/92	removed fish line from lower unit	4330	—	self
9/30/92	new lower unit seal	4360	$111.40	Steven's Marine
10/20/92	winter layup: fog cylinders, fuel stabilizers	4366	$94.60	ditto; didn't change lower unit
10/22/92	paint touch-up	4366	—	self; need recoat in spring
4/10/90	spring launch	4366	$88.40	engine oil

Figure 9-1 Sample logs *(continued on the following page)*.

Daily Engine Log

Date	10/21/90		
Engine hours	412-440		
Oil added	1 qt. (30W)		
Fuel consumption		approx. 135 gal.	
Distance traveled		approx. 70 miles	

Gauges after warm-up

IDLE RPM	WATER PRESS.	ENG. TEMP.	VOLTS
750	40 psi	175	14.5

Observations	hard starting

Daily Engine Log

Date	10/24/90		
Engine hours	440-443		
Oil added	none		
Fuel consumption		approx. 60 gal.	
Distance traveled		approx. 20 miles	

Gauges after warm-up

IDLE RPM	WATER PRESS.	ENG. TEMP.	VOLTS
750	40 psi	175	14.5

Observations	none

Daily Engine Log

Date	10/29/90		
Engine hours	443-449		
Oil added	none (change 10/27)		
Fuel consumption		approx. 35 gal.	
Distance traveled		approx. 20 miles	

Gauges after warm-up

IDLE RPM	WATER PRESS.	ENG. TEMP.	VOLTS
750	40 psi	175	14.5

Observations	tune-up at 443 hours; starts fine

much oil your engine consumes over a period of time, and oil consumption is the single most significant index of your engine's overall health.

Fuel consumption is another significant index of engine health. When fuel consumption increases, there's always a reason. It might be a heavier load, higher operating speeds, wear, or a faulty component. Unless you have a fuel flow meter on board, you'll need to calculate your fuel mileage by combining estimates of average speed, distance traveled, time underway, and fuel used inferred from how much it takes to top off your tank. Do all your estimates in your logbook so you'll have a record of this data.

Admittedly this will produce a less than precise figure; still it will be sufficiently accurate to be meaningful. If you're proficient at dead reckoning (getting a fix by estimating time, course, and speed), your estimation of total fuel consumption is likely to be surprisingly accurate.

Gauge Readings

You should make note of the readings of your most important gauges at start-up, again when the engine has reached operating speed, and just before you shut it down. Among the parameters you'll make note of are idle speed, engine oil pressure, coolant temperature, and even battery voltage.

Obviously you can carry this kind of thing so far that you'll never leave the dock, but even a complete inventory should take no more than a couple of minutes. To save time and space, use shorthand. For instance, if your engine produces 60 pounds of oil pressure when cold and 40 pounds when hot, you could write it: oil 60 lb.-C/40 lb.-H.

The purpose of accumulating all this data is to establish an operating baseline, a list of criteria that constitute the typical operating characteristics of your engine. This can be particularly valuable when you have to call a mechanic, but it also can be valuable because it establishes an operational trend. For instance, if you look at your log for the last 100 hours and note that at the beginning your engine typically ran at 180°F and today it runs at 195°F, you'd have reason to be concerned. Such an increase by itself wouldn't be sufficient to alarm most mechanics nor would it trip an alarm system, but if engine load or operating speed hasn't changed drastically, you'd have to suspect the possibility of a cooling system problem.

Observations

As we'll see in subsequent chapters, you can tell a great deal about the state of your engine by observing certain physical signs, such as the color of its exhaust, the smoothness with which it idles and runs, how easy or difficult it is to start, the presence of oil or fluid in the bilge, and yes, even the noises it makes. After you've spent a few hours at the wheel you'll develop a certain "feel" for your engine, just as commercial boaters do, and you'll know when something doesn't seem quite right. Your observations of your propulsion system are important, if not at the moment, then as indicators of future trends. Write them down; some day they'll come in handy.

Ambient Temperature and Humidity

You can't properly interpret all the raw data noted above unless you know the ambient (outside your boat) conditions. Why? Because both temperature and humidity have a direct effect on how your engine operates. If you don't know how cold it was when you noted that the engine was hard to start, the observation is far less meaningful. Likewise, if you don't recall that when your engine was operating at 190°F you were in the Bahamas and the water temperature was 88°F, that observation has little meaning.

How do you get such information? The easiest way is simply to tune your VHF to a weather channel (which you should do before you start any day aboard a boat) and listen to the NOAA reports, which periodically provide current air temperature and humidity—usually also water temperature, which is important because it directly affects the operating temperature of raw-water cooled engines. It also affects the efficiency of heat exchangers in fresh-water cooled engines.

All things being equal, the higher the ambient air temperature, the less horsepower your engine will produce. Since hot air is less dense, less oxygen reaches the combustion chamber per stroke. Note that the same is true if it's cool outside but hot (due to insufficient ventilation) in your engine compartment.

Again you can record this information quickly in shorthand. If the air temperature is 90°F, the humidity is 80 percent, and the water temperature is 86°F, write AT90/H80/WT86. And by the way, this information also can be valuable when planning a cruise or fishing in familiar waters.

The Daily Checklist

Yes, it's a pain. You'd much rather just fire up that engine and head off into the sunrise. You've dealt with enough hassles during the week; now's the time to relax. But don't. Just take a few minutes—that's all it will take—to make a few crucial checks. Those few minutes are essential to your preventative maintenance program. They will help ensure that your trip really will be hassle-free. Make yourself a short checklist, including the following items, and post it in a prominent place or in your log, so you don't forget.

Check Your Oil

You may have done it just yesterday, but do it again today and every morning before you shove off. It is entirely possible that during the last few hours of running something went wrong—maybe your mechanic forgot to tighten your oil filter—and you're down to your last few quarts of oil. Just two or three more hours of running and that oil pump will start sucking air, and there you go: burned bearings, busted trip, and big repair dollars.

Just pull the dip stick, wipe it off with a clean cloth, punch it back in, and note its reading. Then stop for a moment and think: Is it significantly lower than yesterday? If it is, make a note of it in your log. Perhaps you'll want to check it again at midday when you drop the hook for lunch, just to see if it's gotten any worse. Just remember to wait about 10 minutes between shutdown and checking to allow most of the oil to drain back into the oil pan. Otherwise you'll get an erroneously low reading on your dip stick.

If you've been keeping a log, you know where your engine oil level normally runs on the dip stick. If you haven't, it may fool you. For some reason—no one seems to know why—some engines simply will not run at the full mark on the stick. If that's the case with your engine, make a note of it in your log. If it's a chronic operating condition (and you're sure it is), you may want to go so far as scratching a second full mark on the dip stick to signify the "normal" operating level.

Check Coolant Level

If your engine is fresh-water cooled, the proper amount of coolant level is crucial to its health. If the level drops significantly, the circulating pump will begin to suck air, forming air bubbles in the coolant. Each bubble will become a hot spot, and eventually your engine will overheat.

In the world of engines, one of the greatest inventions is also one of the simplest: the **coolant recovery bottle**. Today, most fresh-water cooled engines are equipped with this simple, translucent plastic container that tells you the level of coolant in the engine without your ever removing a cap. If your engine doesn't have a coolant recovery bottle, either purchase one and install it yourself or have your mechanic install one. With it in place, all you need do is cast a glance toward the bottle and note whether the level falls somewhere between the "high" and "low" marks. If it does, your job is done.

If it doesn't, top it off and note the fact in your log. Frequent topping off can indicate either a leak or an engine that is overheating—and maybe a boater who isn't watching the temperature gauge (it also could mean a faulty gauge).

Whatever the reason, when you top off make sure you add the same type of coolant that is already in the engine. Typically, this is a mixture of half antifreeze and half water, but your engine may be different. Be aware of what is in the system, make up a gallon container of it, and keep it on board so you can keep the level where it should be. If you or your mechanic has added a rust preventative to the cooling system, be aware that it will be diluted each time you top off. Refer to your log and when necessary add more product.

As with oil, some engines seem to prefer a level of coolant that may not fall within the two marks on the coolant bottle. If your engine falls into this category, first make certain there is no problem. Then make a note of this fact in your log and don't try to keep the bottle topped off. The coolant will only overflow into the bilge, be pumped out, and pollute the surrounding water. The best solution is simply to re-mark the bottle with levels that your engine prefers.

If your engine has no coolant bottle and you choose not to install one, you'll have to remove the cap to check the fluid level. If you do this daily in the morning before start-up, there will be no problem because your engine will be cold. If it isn't, **use extreme caution when removing the cap.** Even an engine that has been shut down for a couple of hours may still have a pressurized cooling system due to an elevated temperature and concomitant coolant expansion. Not only can pressurized engine coolant burn you, it is also a toxic substance that can, among other things, damage your eyes. To be safe, only check an engine that has sat overnight.

If you're checking your coolant by removing the cap, note that most systems are not designed to be filled to the rim. Check your owner's manual and chances are you'll find that the proper cold level is somewhere from one to two inches below the rim. Stick your finger in; if it comes out wet, everything is probably OK.

One final note about coolant checks: Observe the color of the coolant. Today's antifreezes come in various colors, but you should be alert for any unusual cloudiness or red coloration that may signal incipient corrosion. By checking your log you should know your engine coolant's normal color. If there's any significant variance, it may mean that the system should be flushed and filled with new coolant.

Conduct a General Visual Survey of the Engine

Before you consider your job finished, take a quick look around for signs of trouble, perhaps a pool of oil or coolant, missing paint, or something loose. Grab some of the external components and shake them to make sure they're secure. Make sure the V-belts are tight. Look under the engine, not only for leakage but also for errant bolts and nuts.

Check Your Battery's Electrolyte Level

If your batteries are difficult to get to this can be a real task. You may have to resort to a mirror and flashlight to get a good reading, but even if you must, don't skip this checkpoint. Make sure you know what the proper electrolyte level is; too much can be as bad as too little. A good rule of thumb is that the level should be about halfway between the top of the plates and the top of the battery. And while you're there, check that the battery is securely mounted, that there is no sign of fluid around it (an indication of a cracked battery case), and that the terminals are not corroded or dirty. Be careful; battery electrolyte is an acid that can harm you and your boat.

Log It

Write down the results of your checks in your log, even if everything is normal. Just knowing precisely when you last checked over your engine and precisely what you did can be a valuable advantage in the battle to keep your boat running smoothly.

The Daily Checklist: A Summary

❏ **Oil**
Wait at least 10 minutes after shutdown; check log to determine trends.

❏ **Coolant (fresh water)**
If engine is equipped with recovery bottle, check level visually. If engine has no recovery bottle, wait until engine has cooled overnight before removing coolant cap to check. Look for discoloration. Be sure to add type and mixture of coolant already in the engine.

❏ **Battery**
Check electrolyte level, mountings, and for signs of leaking.

❏ **General**
Look for oil or coolant leaks, loose parts, parts in the drip pan, frayed belts, soft hoses, or anything out of the ordinary.

❏ **Log**
Whatever action you take, note it in the log.

The Periodic Checklist

For day-to-day operation, the simple daily check detailed in the previous chapter is sufficient, but every 30 days or 20 hours of engine time, you should spend a little more time in the engine compartment, checking things with a closer eye. Again, even this more thorough perusal should take only a little of your time—maybe 20 minutes.

Before you start, you'll need a few simple tools. One of the most important is a flashlight, preferably one that throws a small, high-intensity beam. Also important are a rubber-tipped hammer, a flat-blade screwdriver, and an adjustable wrench.

Periodic checks are best conducted when the engine has sat idle overnight. You'll be crawling around and touching many of the components, which will be hot if the engine's been running. Wear a pair of coveralls or at least some old clothing. And finally, bring along a note pad, or better yet your logbook, so you can record your observations.

Examine the Oil

The first step in the periodic check is to conduct the five-point daily checklist presented in the previous chapter. However, this time when you check your oil take the time to observe it more closely for signs of coolant contamination. Any liquid in oil usually shows up iridescent in strong light, so your flashlight will come in handy here.

You cannot determine how clean or dirty your oil is by looking at it, because today's high-detergent oils are designed to turn black almost immediately after use. The only way to really determine the condition of your oil is to draw a sample of it and send it out for an oil analysis. Analysis is available from a variety of laboratories (usually listed in the Yellow Pages under "Laboratories, Spectrographic") or from a local engine repair facility.

If you're really serious about engine maintenance, have your engine oil analyzed once a year, preferably at the end of the season. It's cheap—no more than $10—and the report you receive will tell you in easy-to-understand language everything from how fast your engine is wearing to whether it's blown a head gasket.

Test the Coolant

If your engine is fresh-water cooled, you'll also be checking your coolant as part of your daily test. For this check you'll need a **coolant tester**, an inexpensive (less than $10) syringe-like device that tells at a glance the concentration of antifreeze in your engine's cooling system. Antifreeze contains rust inhibitors that are crucial to your engine's health, but the effectiveness of these and all the additives in antifreeze degrade over time, eventually leaving your engine unprotected. An antifreeze tester is the only way you can check the potency of your engine coolant. If the reading falls below the recommended minimum, top off with some fresh coolant.

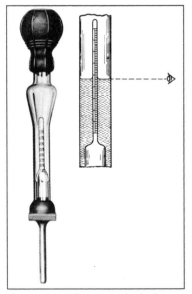

Figure 11-1 A battery testing hydrometer, and its close cousin the coolant tester, can paint an accurate portrait of your battery's state of charge (or your coolant's level of protection) at a glance.

Check Your Battery's State of Charge

You'll be checking the fluid level in your battery again, but this time more thoroughly. The syringe-like **hydrometer**, which will indicate the state of charge in each battery cell, is the tool of choice here. This is important because your battery may read 12 volts or higher on a voltmeter and yet one cell may be significantly weaker than the others, pointing toward trouble down the road. Even the best hydrometers (those that compensate for temperature) won't cost more than $20 and are simple to use. Keep one on board.

Check the Plumbing

At this point you'll begin a more comprehensive check of your engine. The first things you should check are hoses and clamps. Squeeze the hoses. A good hose should be firm and resilient. A broken down one will feel mushy and collapse easily under pressure; it should be replaced. Use your flashlight to look for signs of peeling, cracking, or other external indications of breakdown.

Test clamps with your screwdriver to ensure they're tight. If you find one that isn't, tighten it, but be careful: these clamps strip easily. As a safety measure, all hoses, especially those carrying raw water, should be double-clamped. Don't forget to check the hoses that pass through the transom plate.

Check any through-hull fittings for leaks and signs of wear. Open and close any sea cocks to ensure they work easily. Note that some types have Zerk-style grease fittings and require lubrication with a grease gun about every 90 days.

Check the Electrical System

Next check all electrical wiring, with special attention to **terminals** and **connections**. Check for looseness by pulling gently on the wire or plug—you'd rather have it come apart here than somewhere out in the ocean. Make temporary repairs with twist connectors and electrician's tape, permanent repairs require clamp-style electrical connectors or soldered junctions covered with heat-sensitive shrink wrap.

Selectively tighten terminals with your screwdriver. Look for dangling wires and support them at closely spaced intervals with either tape or tie-wraps. Look for signs of chafing where wiring passes through bulkheads or around metal components. Any loss of insulation, even if the wire isn't exposed, demands repair and preventative measures to see that it doesn't get worse.

Check the high-tension wires, those leading from the coil to the distributor and distributor to each spark plug. **Do not pull them out**! This will weaken the terminal. Grasp each firmly and wiggle it, looking for signs of looseness or weakness. Also look for signs of frayed insulation and make sure all wires are supported and clear of any hot engine parts.

Check Fuel Lines

Next turn your attention to the rubber fuel line leading to the fuel pump. Trace it back as far as you can, looking for abrasions, breaks, loose fittings, or leaks. (Remember that gasoline evaporates quickly so your only clue may be odor from the residue.) Check as far as you can visually using your flashlight, then rely on feel. Any rough spot should be suspect. And while you're groping around, be careful of loose strands of fiberglass and exposed screw heads that can wreak havoc on your hands.

A leak in the hard steel fuel line that runs from the fuel pump to the carburetor is highly unlikely, but you should give it a quick look anyway. Look here for signs of "weeping" at connection points. Check also for leaks around the oil filter (usually visible as drips on the bottom of the filter). If you have a remote-mounted oil filter, examine around the hose connections.

Check Your Engine's Physical Condition

Your visual inventory needs to include the engine mounts. Look for any signs of looseness and be especially watchful for cracks developing around the fiberglass in the forward engine mounts. Rap them a few times with your rubber hammer to ensure they're solid.

Next check over your engine's principal components to make sure they're all tight. These may include the heat exchanger, intake and exhaust manifolds, alternator, raw-water pump, power steering pump, and remote oil filter. This is also a good time to check **V-belts** for signs of **glazing** (a slick, polished appearance on the inside of the belt) due to slippage, cracks due to aging, and fraying due to pulley misalignment. A good rule of thumb for belt tightness is that you shouldn't be able to deflect the belt more than ½ inch. If you can, the belt needs tightening. Don't over-tighten; that will place excessive strain on alternator and water-pump bearings.

Less frequently—about every 90 days—remove the zinc pencils from each of your heat exchangers on fresh-water cooled engines and see how much of each is left. Remember, these are supposed to wear away, but if they get much below half gone you should replace them. Don't be alarmed if some water spurts out of the hole left when you remove the zinc. Just put in the replacement if it is necessary.

Make a thorough inspection of all the areas where engine components are attached, looking for signs of leakage. In some engines, a certain amount of oil will weep, particularly around the oil filter cap and valve covers; it is normal. Wipe it off, note it in your logbook, and check it again next time. If your engine is a V, look in the valley between the cylinder banks. Note any significant pooling of coolant or oil, and don't forget to look under the engine as well.

Clean Up

Leave your engine and engine compartment as clean and free of oil and grease as possible. A clean environment makes it easier to spot oil or coolant leaks. Likewise, touch up any chipped paint or bare metal with an approved paint designed to withstand high temperatures. Not only will it make your engine look nicer, it also will help resist corrosion and make real problems easier to spot.

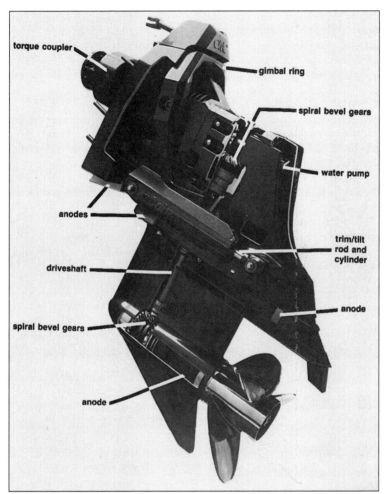

Figure 11-2 Your periodic checkpoints should include all zinc anodes, the trim/tilt cylinders, and the water pump. The pump on the OMC Cobra is easy to access. (Courtesy OMC)

The Drive Unit

Now turn your attention to the drive unit itself. There are only four check points here, but they are important. First, check the level of lube oil in the lower unit. In most drive units this means unscrewing a plug with a screwdriver and making sure some either dribbles out or you can at least feel it with your finger. Be careful! There are usually two plugs. The lower is for draining only; you want the upper one.

At the same time note the color of the lube oil. If it's cloudy, you've got a leak, probably around the propeller seal. Have it fixed immediately or you'll soon have serious drive unit problems. Finally, screw the plug back in, making sure it's tight.

Second, check the condition of the zincs you can see, usually the one on the top of the lower unit and the one under the transom shield. As long as each is intact you're OK. But again, you're looking for trends. If one of your zincs has dissolved a lot since your last check, it's a sure sign you've got a corrosion problem. Check it out.

Third, look for nicks and scrapes on the drive unit. Touch up any with approved touch-up paint to prevent them from turning into corrosion problems.

Fourth, make a general inspection, looking for leakage around the trim cylinders, loose parts or wires, or any obvious damage.

And finally, make sure to note any observations of conditions, whether you made repairs or not, in your log.

The Periodic Checklist: A Summary

❑	**Oil**	Check level; send out sample for analysis annually.
❑	**Coolant**	Check level, check potency with coolant tester.
❑	**Battery**	Check electrolyte level, mountings, leakage, and state of charge in each cell with a hydrometer.
❑	**Hoses**	Look for leaks or deterioration (hoses should be firm, not mushy); check for loose or corroded clamps.
❑	**Electrical**	Test for loose terminals, check for sealed connections; look for frayed wiring and worn insulation.
❑	**Fuel Lines**	Check hard lines; look for abrasion on soft lines; look for weeping at connections.
❑	**Soft Lines**	Check all clamped lines for tightness and integrity.
❑	**Engine Mounts**	Look for signs of looseness; look for cracks in fiberglass mounting points.
❑	**Miscellaneous**	Check for tightness of heat exchanger (if so equipped), intake manifold, exhaust manifold, alternator, and raw-water pump.

❑	**V-Belts**	Look for fraying or glazing; check for proper tightness (½ inch of play).
❑	**Zincs**	Replace any that are more than half gone.
❑	**Leaks**	Check the oil pan, vents, hoses and lines, gaskets, all mating surfaces, cylinder valley (V-engines).
❑	**Drive unit**	Check lube oil level and color. Check and touch up nicks. Check condition of zincs. Conduct overall examination.
❑	**Log**	Note anything out of the ordinary in your log.

From Start-Up to Shutdown

The few minutes immediately after you start a stern drive and just before you shut it down are the most crucial times in its life. How you treat it during that time will, in large part, determine how long your stern drive lasts.

Start-Up

After you've completed your preliminary checks and have run the bilge blowers, you're ready to start your engine. You'll notice that many captains "pump" the throttle a few times to "prime" the engine before turning the key. Although it may look authoritative, it is a waste of time and actually may make the engine harder to start by over-fueling it. In most cases, moving the throttle lever all the way forward and back to neutral is all that's needed. This movement causes the accelerator pump to shoot a stream of gas into the carburetor throat and also closes the choke plate if it's open.

Under normal circumstances, pushing the throttle lever forward automatically shifts the stern drive into forward. You want to open the throttle slightly while keeping the stern drive in neutral. (Thanks to a safety mechanism, if you try to start your stern drive while it's in gear the engine will not crank.)

How you do this depends upon whose control you use. If you have a Mercury/Quicksilver, you'll probably find a black button to push in the middle of the lever axis. On many other controls you first pull the base of the lever out, then push it forward. If you're not sure how to advance the throttle in neutral, check your owner's manual.

Opening the throttle gives the engine a little more gasoline and usually makes starting easier. Don't pump the throttle and don't open it

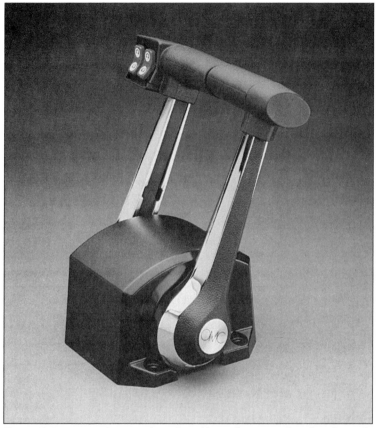

Figure 12-1 Many engine controls, such as this one for two engines, have integral switches for trimming or tilting the engine. To advance the dual throttles while keeping the engines in neutral you must pull on each base. (Courtesy OMC)

too far—about one-third of the way is usually sufficient. Any farther and you'll either flood the engine or the engine will roar to life, which causes undue wear and tear.

With the throttle open and your hand on it, crank the engine over. Keep your hand on the throttle so that when the engine begins to turn over you can throttle back if it roars to life. Your goal should be a fast-idle (which your car does automatically) speed of about 1500 r.p.m.

Once the engine is running, leave it alone. Now is a good time to untie lines, pull in fenders, and do all the last-minute things you must do before shoving off. If you have small children around (or irresponsible adults), it's a good idea to have someone guard the throttle to prevent accidents while you're busy. After about two minutes, pull the throttle back into neutral. The engine should idle down to between 700 and 900 r.p.m. You're now ready to get under way.

If you wait until your engine idles down before you place your stern drive into gear, you'll save a lot of wear and tear. In addition, idling away from the dock for a minute or so allows all the gears to become fully lubricated, which reduces wear. Above all, remember that the highest wear rates in engines and drives occur when they are cold and oil isn't fully circulating. Take it easy and you'll make sure your stern drive lasts.

Trimming your drive all the way down or "in" will help the boat plane more quickly and will reduce engine load. Depress the trim button until you hear the hydraulic pump strain (it's OK; it's designed to do that), make sure the wheel is straight, then apply power smoothly and steadily until your boat is on plane. Once it's there, throttle back or up to your desired cruising speed.

Don't drive your boat at speeds between hull speed and planing if you can avoid it. If your boat is running in an exaggerated nose-high attitude in spite of having the drive trimmed all the way in, either put it up on plane or throttle it back to a speed where you're running more level. Running just off plane places undue strain on your stern drive and causes an unnecessarily large wake that can damage other boats and make other boaters uncomfortable. Your rule of thumb should always be: Minimize wake, even if there doesn't seem to be anyone around. Wakes can travel many miles and still cause damage, and a large wake is a sign of a boat that is running inefficiently and out of trim. For your sake and others', always minimize your wake.

Choosing a Cruising Speed

The next question is at what speed you should cruise. It is widely accepted that the faster you run a gasoline engine, the faster it wears. Fuel efficiency (and thereby range) is always the product of many things, including hull form, but a general rule is that a stern drive will run most efficiently at slightly faster than planing speed. In many cases this means somewhere between 3000 and 3300 r.p.m. Any faster usually produces more speed but lower mileage. Another general rule is that the greater the disparity between speed and mileage, the greater the engine load. The greater the engine load, the higher the wear rate.

On an engine with four-barrel carburetors, the secondary venturis usually open at around 3400 r.p.m. (You should be able to tell when they open by the elevated intake noise level.) Avoid opening the carburetor secondaries and you'll usually save fuel.

Another factor in selecting the best cruising speed is using optimum trim. This is generally a matter of trial and error since it's dependent on variables such as weight, weight distribution, and water conditions. The best way to trim is to push the trim button to the up position until you hear the engine speed up (assuming you're not moving the throttle), then trim it down just a tad until the engine speed drops back. The increase in speed you hear is the propeller losing bite in the water, and what you're aiming for is maximum bite with the bow as high as you can get it without losing control or visibility. When the bow is high, the water drag on the hull is minimized and your boat will run faster and more efficiently. You should notice significantly less steering torque when the drive is properly trimmed.

Shutting Down

The rule here is simple, but often ignored: Give the engine just a little time to cool down before shutting it off. The most prudent course is to reverse the start-up procedure: Pull into the dock or mooring, throttle the engine back to idle, and go about your anchoring/mooring chores for a minute while your engine cools down. Then you can safely shut it off.

Many boaters can't resist that last punch of the throttle to speed up the engine before switching off the key. All that punch does is wear away a little more engine and shoot into the cylinders a little more raw fuel that won't burn completely. That wasted fuel will drip down the cylinder and into the oil where it will dilute the oil's ability to lubricate the engine. In other words, it will cause more wear.

PART THREE

How to Care for Your Stern Drive

Selecting and Changing Oil

This chapter is not meant to contradict in any way the maintenance schedule and manufacturer's recommendations included in your owner's manual. On the contrary, it is complementary, and is intended to help you better fulfill those guidelines.

One of the beauties of the modern stern drive is that it is a relatively low-maintenance piece of machinery. It is not unusual for an automotive version of a stern drive engine to log 100,000 miles without a major problem. Mathematically, that translates into more than 10 years of use in a boat; practically it's somewhat less because of the greater average load under which a marine engine must operate. Even so, follow just a few simple maintenance procedures and your engine and drive will far outlive your tenure as its owner. The most important factor in proper marine maintenance is lubrication, and that means choosing the right oil and changing it at the right time.

API Oil Classification

By now you should know that your boat's engine and drive unit must have a clean supply of lubricating oil to run long and well. Equally important is the right type of oil. Engine lubricating oils are classified by the American Petroleum Institute (API) according to the type of engines for which they were designed and the complexity of their additive package. Oils are also classified according to the ease with which they flow at a specific temperature. Two typical combined engine oil ratings are SE 30W and SF-CD 10W-30.

In terms of API classification, there are two types of engines: spark-ignition (gasoline engines) and compression-ignition (diesels). An oil rated "S" is designed for use in a gasoline engine while one rated "C" is meant for diesels. Some oils carry dual ratings, such as SF-CC, meaning the oil can be used either in gasoline or diesel engines.

Always use an oil rated S or S and C in your stern drive engine. Such oils are designed for the specific operating demands and conditions imposed by four-cycle gasoline engines. Other types of oils or oils that carry no rating may cause severe damage and accelerated wear to your engine. If the API classification is not clearly visible on the outside of each oil container, select another brand.

The second letter of the API designation represents the complexity of the additive package, typically starting with A, the lowest level with the least advanced additives, and progressing upward alphabetically. It is not important to know precisely what additive package is represented by each letter. All you need to know is this simple rule: Always choose the highest letter available. In other words, if you have a choice between SE or SG, choose SG, regardless of what type of engine you have.

At this time the highest available classification for spark-ignition engines is SG, but lubricating oils are always being researched and improved, and as soon as a better additive package is discovered it will no doubt be implemented and the oil using it will be designated SH. As long as you use the highest-rated oil available, you can't go wrong.

Viscosity Classification

There is one other factor to consider when selecting oil: its ability to flow freely at a specific temperature, a characteristic commonly referred to as its weight or viscosity. Viscosity is designated by an arbitrary number, usually between 5 and 50. The lower the number, the thinner the oil and the easier it will flow when cold. But low-viscosity oil also is less likely to maintain successfully the proper oil film at high temperatures. Higher numbers indicate a thicker, more viscous oil that does not flow as easily when cold but is less likely to become excessively thin when hot.

Some oils carry two viscosity designations, such as 10W-30 (the W stands for weight); these are called multi-viscosity oils. A 10W-30 oil has the thickness of a 10-weight oil when it is cold and a 30-weight oil when it is hot. Sound ideal? Some engine builders believe that because more additives must go into the oil to achieve multi-viscosity, some of the oil's lubricative properties must be displaced, reducing engine protection. True or not, most builders recommend single-viscosity oil for stern drives in pleasure-boat operation.

The question of single- versus multi-weight oil generally is a moot one anyway because most pleasure boats are not operated either in extremely cold or extremely hot environments, where "multi-vis" oils have a distinct advantage. Under typical ambient conditions, a single-weight oil, usually a 30W, is sufficient. In any case, check your owner's manual and adhere to its recommendations.

Most engine builders do not recommend mixing oils of different viscosities unless it is absolutely necessary. For this reason it's always wise to carry on board a few one-quart cans of the same oil that's in your engine. Of course, if you must add a quart, note it in your log.

When it comes time to change oil you—not your mechanic—should decide what kind of oil goes into your engine. Follow the manufacturer's guidelines strictly, and if you have a question, don't hesitate to call the manufacturer or distributor. For instance, if your engine is using a lot of oil between changes, it may help to go to a heavier weight. But before you do, consult an engine expert to make sure higher-viscosity oil still can do the job at cold start-up.

Oil-Change Interval

Speaking of changing oil, many boat owners are unsure how often it should be done. Since oil changes are bothersome and sometimes messy, most boat owners don't want to change too frequently, yet most are aware that an oil change is the single most effective thing they can do to prolong the life of their engine.

To determine the proper oil-service interval, start with your owner's manual. Its recommendation should be the outside limit only; unusual conditions may warrant less time between oil changes. If your engine has been run unusually hard, has spent a lot of time at idle speeds where it could not always warm up fully, or has been subject to any other unusual operating condition (dust, heavy loads, constant starting and stopping), reduce the interval between oil changes. Note also that, even when oil sits in an engine that has not been run, you should change it periodically since various acids, moisture, and other contaminants will accumulate in it. Clearly there's a certain amount of guesswork involved in deciding exactly when to change oil. If you find that bothersome, there is an alternative: oil analysis (see Chapter 11). Otherwise, err on the safe (frequent) side.

One final note about oil changes. You may be tempted to change the filter less frequently than the oil—perhaps only every other oil change—because it's difficult to reach or to save a little money. Don't! An oil filter is designed not only to trap dirt but to absorb moisture and other liquid contaminants. At oil-change time the filter contains well over a quart of dirty oil that can immediately reduce the benefit of the oil change for which you just paid so dearly by as much as one-fourth. Change the filter every time you change the oil. It's cheap insurance.

Additives

As soon as you purchase a stern drive someone will try to sell you an additive to vastly improve the quality of your oil, or even to free you of the drudgery of changing oil altogether. Engine builders almost universally agree that oil additives are a waste of money. Today's oils contain the best additives available; putting anything more into them will do little or no good, and might actually cause harm by interfering with the very carefully conceived and executed additive package.

Face it: Oil and a good filter are cheap protection. Money spent on them today is money in the bank down the road.

Drive Unit Oil

Like your stern drive engine, your drive unit also needs a supply of oil to keep its moving parts (mainly gears) from wearing out. This oil, however, is totally different in weight and constitution from engine oil. This is gear oil, a heavier-weight lube specifically designed to coat and protect gears.

Check your owner's manual for drive oil recommendations. Chances are your unit will require "hypoid" oil or similar. If you want to play it safe you can simply purchase the oil sold under the name of your drive's builder. There are also many fine after-market oils that are equally effective. Just make sure you pick the oil your drive unit needs.

Under most operating conditions, drive oil need only be changed once each season. However, as noted previously, you should periodically check the oil level in your drive and its clarity, which will tell you if it has become contaminated with water. These checks are important because if there's a problem with leakage between oil and water you'll likely never know unless you see it manifested in a lower oil level or cloudy oil. Left alone, either low oil or water-contaminated oil will ruin your drive unit.

Caring for Fuel

Gasoline is a complex substance with a number of important properties, but only a few concern us. One is octane, a measure of the fuel's ability to resist ignition before the spark plug fires. Generally, the higher the compression ratio, the higher the octane required to prevent pre-ignition. Fortunately, today most engines run just fine on regular-octane fuel.

If you have an older, high-compression or special high-performance engine, you may need to purchase higher octane fuel. One sign that your engine needs higher octane fuel is that it knocks or pings when it's under load. Some knock is acceptable, but severe, loud, continuous knock is cause for concern. Knock can also be a sign that the ignition timing is out of adjustment. If your engine knocks constantly and higher octane fuel doesn't seem to help, better check its timing and dwell.

Another property of gasoline that's important to boaters is the presence of alcohol. Alcohol can come from a variety of sources such as grains and wood. It's usually added to extend gasoline and reduce costs. Alcohol has two properties that concern boaters: (1) It can attract and combine with water in a damp environment, meaning less power and more fuel system corrosion; (2) It can attack certain kinds of synthetic rubber fuel lines, usually those in older boats.

If you have an older boat you should be especially attentive during your regular check of fuel line components. Look for sticky or soft lines, or lines that remain depressed when you squeeze them. Replace these with new fuel lines, nearly all of which are now rated for use with alcohol fuels.

The best defense against moisture is to keep your fuel tank full

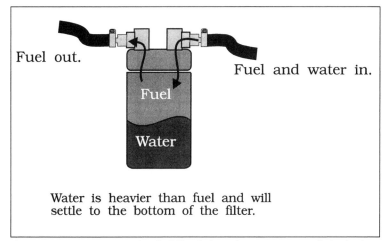

Fuel out.

Fuel and water in.

Fuel

Water

Water is heavier than fuel and will settle to the bottom of the filter.

Figure 14-1 A water-separating fuel filter helps reduce water accumulation in the fuel tank. The water that enters the filter is heavier than the fuel so it settles to the bottom of the filter. Only fuel travels to the tank.

when you're not using your boat. This will reduce condensation and water accumulation in the fuel tank. You also can add an auxiliary water-separating fuel filter, available from most engine and boat dealers, and after-market suppliers. Such a filter also keeps dirt out of your fuel system.

That brings us to the final important fuel property: cleanliness. The carburetor contains a number of small passages that easily clog with even the tiniest particulate matter. Likewise, abrasive material, such as sand and grit, that makes its way into the combustion chamber may not be destroyed during combustion and may end up grinding away your rings and cylinder walls.

Most engines have a small particulate filter in the carburetor where the metal fuel line attaches. (You usually have to remove the fuel line and look inside to see it.) Its capacity is small and it's really designed as a filter of last resort. You should have a large canister-type filter somewhere between the engine and the fuel tank to offer real protection. Better yet, make it a water-separating fuel filter like the one described two paragraphs earlier. Most filter elements are good for one boating season and replacement cost is typically less than $10. Once again, cheap insurance.

If your fuel filter does become clogged, your engine will begin to miss as it starves for fuel or, more likely, just quit. The only solution is to replace the contaminated fuel filter, which is a good reason to always carry a spare. In most installations, you will have to fill the fuel filter cartridge with fuel before attaching it to prevent the engine from sucking air.

If your filters are constantly clogging, your problem may not be at the pump; it may be in your fuel tank. Most tanks are designed with the fuel pick-up a few inches off the bottom of the tank. This leaves a dead area in which dirt and heavy contaminants can accumulate without being drawn into the fuel line. If you have an older boat or one with a lot of hours on it your fuel tank may have a layer of contaminant on its bottom that has built up sufficiently to reach the fuel pick-up. The only solution is to have the tank either replaced or cleaned. That's a job for a professional.

Additives

Just as there are dozens of salesmen ready to sell you something to "vastly improve" your oil, so are there plenty of peddlers with "miracle" fuel additives that supposedly will double your mileage. As with after-market oil additives, approach these additives with a healthy dose of skepticism. In most operating environments no fuel additive is necessary and, in some cases, one actually may be harmful. There is, however, one notable exception.

Gasoline is fine as long as it's being used or at least being moved around. When its left idle for long periods, bad things can happen. Moisture and air can combine with it to create oxidation, gum, and varnish that can clog your fuel system.

The solution to fuel oxidation is to add a **fuel stabilizer** whenever you believe your boat will sit undisturbed for more than a month. Fuel stabilizers are formulated to preserve the fuel in its original state. They come in various types and formulations, not all of which are necessarily good for your engine. The best place to turn for advice concerning a fuel stabilizer for your laid-up boat is the engine manufacturer or distributor. Do not rely solely upon advertising claims and don't buy simply what is being sold at the boatyard; there's a lot of snake oil on the market today, some of which can end up taking a big bite out of your wallet while failing to live up to its promises. Companies such as OMC, Mercury Marine, and MDR make reliable fuel stabilizers.

Caring for the Ignition System

I've said it before in this book and I'll say it again: The weakest link in your stern drive engine is its ignition system. That's why you must service and maintain it with diligence. If you don't, you can almost count on problems. Electronic ignitions are not designed to be serviced, only replaced, so we will tackle only mechanical ignition systems in this chapter. Ignition system maintenance comes in two parts: low voltage and high voltage.

Low-voltage maintenance starts at the battery and ends at the coil. Every connection must be clean, tight, and dry or you'll have a current leak. *Clean* means the pole and the connector must each be bright. If they're not, it's not an optimum connection and you should brighten them with a little fine sandpaper. *Tight* is self-explanatory. A loose connection means a weak connection, and weak connections mean trouble.

Dry simply means no moisture. That means you must exclude moisture (and therefore air) by covering each connection (including splices) with an impermeable coating. This could be a special ignition spray or heat-sensitive shrink-wrap. It does not mean merely slide-in, crimp, or twist connectors, nor does it mean the application (in any amount) of just tape or silicone sealant. **Every connection must be air- and moisture-tight or you will have problems.**

High-voltage maintenance starts at the coil and ends at the spark plugs. Remember, you're dealing with as much as 40,000 volts and current that's ever ready to take the shortest way home. If there is any gap or opening to the air, high-voltage current will jump it and go to ground; the spark plug won't fire.

The most critical links in the system are the spark plug wires, in-

Figure 15-1 Spark plug wires are the critical links in the ignition system. The terminal will become loose after a few removals.

cluding their connectors at each end. There can be no exposed or eroded insulation, and all connectors must be tight. The boots that fit over the terminals at the coil, distributor, and spark plugs must be supple and clean. If they're hard, they'll crack and let in air. Air means moisture and moisture means a short circuit. If they're dirty, the dirt will also conduct the high-voltage current to ground and the spark plug won't fire.

If you have any doubt about the condition of your spark plug wires, replace them. If one is bad, the rest are probably soon to go. Opinions vary, but most mechanics like to replace a spark plug wire set every other boating season. The cost shouldn't be more than $50, and you can easily install them yourself.

The next link in the high-voltage chain is the distributor cap. This is the one high-voltage ignition item that's most often overlooked and most often troublesome. The smallest (even invisible) crack and you'll have a short circuit. If the contacts on the inside of the cap are worn, you'll have poor or no connection. If the inside of the cap is covered with grease and grime, you'll probably have a short or cross-firing between poles. Like so many ignition parts, distributor caps are cheap—less than $10. Replace them every season and be safe.

Finally we come to the parts everyone knows about, those that comprise the tune-up. Of course we're speaking of the plugs, points, and condenser. (If you've got a stern drive with electronic ignition, you're off the hook for the points and condenser.) As for points, know that the gap between them must be very accurate. An error of just a few thousandths of an inch will mean arcing, pitting, additional wear, and eventual misfiring. If you can't set the points accurately (and many of us cannot), let a mechanic do it. This is one of the most crucial adjustments in the ignition system. It's got to be right.

If you do install and adjust your own points, consider buying an **electronic dwell meter**. It can tell you far more accurately than mechanical feeler gauges whether your points are set right. Dwell meters are easy to use; just follow the directions that come with them. And by all means, remember to tighten the screws that hold the points securely. One of the most common ignition-related problems—believe it or not—is points that vibrate loose and stop the engine.

You may think that you can save money by purchasing a small file and filing the ridges and peaks on the points, then resetting them. **Don't try it!** Points are cheap. Install a new pair at the beginning of every boating season. Period! And always install a new condenser when you put in the new points.

The story on spark plugs is not as straightforward as it is on points and condenser. With unleaded fuel, spark plugs can easily last three or four boating seasons. If you decide to stretch out their life, you must pull them once a year and re-set the gap between the electrodes. (Check your owner's manual for recommended clearance.) You will also need to clean off the plug tips with a bronze or relatively soft wire brush and clean the white insulator and nut head with a dry, clean cloth. Don't use solvent; it will leave a film and attract more grease and dirt. You could, of course, play it safe and simply replace your spark plugs at the end of every season. That, in my opinion, is not a bad idea.

Whichever option you choose, make sure you remove and install the spark plug wire carefully or you'll have a bad connection and all your work will be for naught. I do one wire at a time so I'm sure to get the right wire connected to the right plug. Once the connector and boot are on the plug, wiggle them to make sure they're snug.

16

Doing It Yourself

For a variety of reasons, including saving money and the simple joy of doing it yourself, a lot of boaters would prefer to do the maintenance chores on their stern drives. Unfortunately many shy away from the task, not because of laziness but because of concern that the job may be too difficult. In truth, the procedures involved in maintaining a stern drive aren't really much different from those used in maintaining your automobile.

Oil

We've already discussed how to choose the right oil; now let's talk about how to change it. First, never change oil when it's cold: It won't flow freely and it will be difficult to get all the dirty oil out of the engine and stern drive. The oil needn't be hot—warm is fine.

When you want to change the oil in your automobile, you simply slide a container under the oil pan, remove the drain plug, and let the oil run out. That procedure is unlikely to work in most stern drive boats because you probably can't get to the drain plug to begin with, and there probably isn't a flat spot under the engine on which you could set a container.

One solution is to pump the warm oil out of the oil pan through the dipstick hole. Most newer stern drives have made a provision for this by threading a fitting onto the end of the tube into which the dip stick fits. You simply remove the dipstick, thread a hose to this fitting, and pump the warm oil out of the engine.

On older stern drives not equipped with this fitting, you'll have to snake a hose down the dipstick hole, making sure that you don't push the hose too far or it will curl up in the pan and out of the oil. In either case, the mechanism commonly used for pumping is a simple **centrifugal pump** that fits on the end of an electric drill. Its advantages are low cost and portability. Due to its small size, however, its power is limited. Another disadvantage is that you need a supply of 120-volt current to power it.

Another solution is a **12-volt pump**, which has a supply cable that simply clamps to your battery's terminal via alligator clips. It's more powerful but larger and more expensive. A third alternative, usually found only in larger boats, is a permanently-mounted oil change system.

Once you have a container full of dirty oil, you have to find a way to dispose of it responsibly. This can be a real problem in some places, although many states now require anyone who sells oil to accept used oil in return. This shouldn't even require mentioning, but unfortunately it does: Don't pour the oil on the ground, down the sewer, or into the water. It will only end up polluting the environment.

Many boat owners pour the used oil back into the oil containers and store them in a safe place until their municipality has an annual "Amnesty Day," in which toxic chemicals are accepted for disposal. Some service stations and recycling centers accept used oil, and there are oil-recovery firms in many urban areas; check your Yellow Pages under "Oils—Waste." With a little perseverance, you can find a proper place to get rid of your oil.

Oil Filter

Chances are you're familiar with your car's spin-on oil filter, a metal canister designed to be discarded completely when removed. The filter on your stern drive engine is precisely the same unit. Indeed, here's one instance where, if you can buy one cheaper at an auto supply store, you can substitute the automotive for the marine with no problem. Just make sure you've got the right filter. If you have any doubt, bring the old one to the auto supply store and the clerk will look up the model number for you on a cross-reference chart.

Removal and installation are the same as with your car: Use a special **oil filter wrench** to remove the old one. Coat the rubber gasket on the new one with fresh oil, then screw it on until the gasket contacts the metal mating surface. Then turn it another three-quarters of a turn to seal it. An added step you may want to consider is filling the filter or canister with clean oil before you install it. Many mechanics do this because it keeps the engine from running dry for the first few seconds after an oil change. If you choose to do the same, remember to keep track of how much oil you add. Overfilling an engine with oil can be both messy and dangerous.

After you change the filter be sure the exterior of the filter is absolutely clean so you'll be able to detect any leakage quickly. If you do your own maintenance on your car, you may be used to a somewhat dirty engine, a fact of life because it's exposed to road grime. Dirt should never be tolerated on a marine engine. The engine, all its components, and the surrounding environment (including the bilge) should be scrupulously clean, not only to help you determine when something is wrong but for safety reasons as well. Remember, your car's engine is exposed to the open air; your boat's engine operates in a relatively closed environment where sloppiness can lead to pollution, slips, and even fire.

Once you have installed the oil filter, start the engine and let it run long enough for the oil to warm. Check for leaks. If there are none, this part of your job is finished—except, of course, for finding a proper way to dispose of the dirty oil filter.

Fuel Filters

As we noted before, most carburetors have a small internal fuel filter where the fuel line enters it. Except under extraordinary circumstances, this should never need cleaning. Many older stern drives have no other fuel filter, a risky proposition. If your engine didn't come with one, you should install one, preferably one of the water-separating types.

Fuel filters usually require changing once a year. There are a number of types—spin-on, cartridge, and in-line—and all are easy to remove and install. However, when you install a new fuel filter you should fill it with clean fuel so the carburetor won't suck air when you start the engine.

Be obsessively vigilant regarding fuel leaks. Gasoline is extremely dangerous. Always make a thorough check for fuel leaks after installing a new fuel filter.

Ignition System

We've already discussed the basics of the stern drive ignition system, but let's go over each part individually from a self-service angle. Once a year you'll need to replace the ignition points and condenser, unless your engine has electronic ignition. If you're steady and precise you can do this, but accuracy in setting points is crucial. You can use a mechanical feeler gauge, but you'll probably get better accuracy using a dwell meter. While you are at this, replace the distributor cap and rotor.

Anyone with a modicum of mechanical ability should be able to remove, clean, gap, and reinstall a set of spark plugs, or gap and install a new set. Just remember to gap them carefully according to the engine manufacturers recommendations. Don't overtighten them.

Once a year, as part of your ignition service, you also should check the engine's ignition timing. This can be a difficult job for a novice, as it requires accurate use of a timing light. If you've never used a timing light, you should have someone show you how to connect one and use it, preferably on your engine. You can get general guidance from a number of automotive books.

Other Service

After oil and filter, the only other periodic service required by your stern drive engine might be cleaning the flame arrestor around the oil filler cap. Also, top off all fluids, including in the power steering pump, if so equipped. The primary cautions here are to use only the approved fluids and solvents, which should be listed in your owner's manual.

Some older stern drives may also have grease fittings or other lubrication points, such as at the throttle linkage. Again, check your owner's manual for specifications.

Winter Lay-Up

If you live where temperatures fall below freezing, you may have to prepare your stern drive for winter lay-up. This is another procedure you either can do yourself or leave to a mechanic. Basically, winterization involves removing any water (not coolant) from the engine cooling system, ensuring that the coolant is of suf-

Figure 16-1 One good way to keep your stern drive well maintained is to use flushers like the one shown here to keep internal cooling passages clear and clean. You can connect this model to a garden hose to run water through the system, recommended after a saltwater cruise. (Courtesy Atwood Corp.)

ficient concentration to protect against freezing, changing the oil and filter, topping off the fuel tanks to prevent condensation, and adding a fuel stabilizer. You also should pull each spark plug and spray rust preventative into the hole. You can buy rust preventative from your local dealer or marine supply store. OMC, Mercury Marine, and MDR make reliable ones. For more specific recommendations, check your engine owner's manual.

The Drive Unit

Regular maintenance on the drive unit is simple. First is the annual drive oil change. Make sure the drive is warm so the oil will flow, trim it all the way down, place a pan beneath it to catch the oil, remove the top screw (the one by which you checked oil level), and finally, remove the bottom screw. Give the lube plenty of time to drain, then replace the lower screw. (This is a good time to check the lube oil for water contamination.)

Most drive lube comes in a tube, whose nozzle fits into the upper fill hole. Cut the end of this nozzle off, insert it into the fill hole, and squeeze until you see oil begin to drip back out, indicating the drive is full. Insert and tighten the plug and properly dispose of the old lube.

Other service involves touching up paint and replacing the zincs that are more than half gone. Make sure you look for subsurface bubbling, a sign that corrosion has entered at one place and traveled between alloy and paint. These areas should be scraped clean, primed, and painted.

If the drive will be out of the water for any time, hose off its exterior to remove salt and contaminants. You may want to apply a coat of wax to protect the drive even further. This is also a good time to flush the drive unit with fresh water using a special adapter that clamps around the raw-water intakes.

If your boat operates in salt water and its zincs show virtually no wear, it may be a sign they aren't doing their job. Look for corrosion in a component that does not have a good connection to the rest of the drive. And never paint or wax zincs.

At this time you may also want to remove the propeller and shine a light inside to check on the condition of the internal zinc in the lower unit. Make sure to reinstall the propeller with a new lock washer. You might also want to pull the propeller and place fresh grease on the prop shaft splines. This will ensure that the prop comes off easily and you won't have to resort to pounding on the prop to loosen it, which could damage the critical prop seals.

Make sure the bright steel hydraulic rams on the trim cylinders have a coat of oil on them. They depend on frequent uses to maintain the coating, and if the coating degrades, the rams will rust and the hydraulic fluid will leak out.

How to Choose and Deal with a Mechanic

Selecting a mechanic is like selecting a physician: You don't really want one but you know you need one, and you're unsure about how to choose one because you don't know much about the discipline. This is why doctors—and mechanics—named Adams fare better than those named Zimmerman: The natural tendency is to rely on alphabetical order when all else fails.

There are ways to tell good mechanics from bad, but shopping for the best deal is not one of them. There are plenty of good mechanics who charge a low hourly rate and just as many bad ones who charge a high hourly rate. If you find a mechanic who works cheap, he may be so incompetent that it takes him twice as long to do the job. We'll deal more with the financial aspects of mechanics in a moment. Right now, let's talk about selecting a good one.

The first rule of dealing with a mechanic is "Don't be intimidated." It's true, you probably know a lot less about engines and drives than he, but never forget that you're the one paying the bills—you should be in the driver's seat. Never be afraid to ask a mechanic anything or to challenge him when you're dissatisfied with his answer. If you learn just this one thing—deal with a mechanic from a position of strength and authority—you will have gone a long way toward getting your money's worth.

Once you start looking for a mechanic your first source should be word of mouth. If you have a friend with a stern drive–equipped boat, ask him if he's happy with his mechanic. If his stern drive is the same make as yours, so much the better. Also ask the yard foreman, the man who sold you the boat, and those whose boats are moored around you.

If you get a rousing recommendation from any of them, check the guy out. If you get two or three opinions that agree, you're in real luck.

The next step should be to meet with the mechanic before you actually call him for work. Ideally, the meeting will take place at his shop so you can have a look around. Being a mechanic is a dirty job, but that doesn't preclude neatness. If he's a slob and his tool box looks like a kid's toy chest, he's disorganized at best and a poor mechanic at worst. And if he doesn't have time to talk to you, forget him.

When you speak to a mechanic, ask him about his training and experience. Any factory training and certification is a big plus, although no guarantee of success. Recurrent training in specialized areas is a sign that he takes his profession seriously and wants to stay abreast of new developments.

Discuss your specific engine, drive, and boat with him, and note how he listens. A lot of mechanics have little or no respect for an owner, and you can tell from the way they listen. Stay away from them, no matter how expert they may seem, or they'll end up directing your life. If the mechanic expresses some familiarity with your engine or boat, that's a good sign. More important, however, is his overall attitude. Does he seem reasonable, interested, and fairminded, as well as being competent?

In the end, you really need to know more about human nature than engines and drives to choose a mechanic. Don't be afraid to rely on your impressions and instincts. The truth is, a good mechanic is hard to find, and finding one often is as much a matter of serendipity as forethought.

What's a Fair Fee?

Mechanics generally compute their charges one of two ways: One is the standard-rate method where, by referring to a book, a mechanic can estimate how much time it should take (at least theoretically) to perform a certain job. He simply multiplies that time by his hourly rate and gets the estimated charges. If he gets the job done faster you still pay the estimated rate; if it takes longer he'll charge you more. The standard-rate method is most common in large shops.

The other method is simply to multiply how long it takes to actually complete the job by the hourly rate. This sounds simple, but there are variations on the theme. For instance, some mechanics show up at a job cold, with no parts and perhaps not even the correct tools. They then proceed to charge you for the time it takes them to travel to and from the shop or parts house, and if that weren't enough, they may even plug in a markup on the parts. Naturally, a mechanic legitimately could find he needs an unanticipated part or tool after getting into a job, but generally this bare-bones approach is a rip-off.

Evaluating Estimates and Invoices

You should be able to get firm estimates for most scheduled maintenance and for most common types of repairs. But understand that a boat is not like a car: Every installation varies slightly. If it takes a mechanic longer to pull a drive out of your boat because the boatbuilder mounted some overhead structure on top of the engine's valve covers, you'll have to pay for it. If, however, a mechanic refuses to give you any firm estimates for scheduled maintenance, you probably should look for another mechanic.

Although it's probably too late to save you at this point, a look at a mechanic's invoice can tell you a lot about the quality of his work. Check the number of hours posted. It's normal to round off time, but if he's rounding off 2½ hours to 3 hours, you're getting ripped off.

Note the prices for parts. This is where many mechanics really pad their bills. If a price seems too high, don't hesitate to ask about it. If the explanation seems inadequate, call a local parts house and verify the cost. You have to expect some markup, but anything over 25 percent is cause for questioning.

Another potential trouble spot is in the miscellaneous category, sometimes referred to as "shop materials." Originally this was intended to cover incidentals, such as shop towels, grease, and miscellaneous chemicals, but often it develops into just another way to jack up the bill. You shouldn't hesitate to ask about this charge either, particularly if it exceeds $25.

Don't be reticent about asking to see any old parts that were replaced. This is not being rude, it's just being a smart customer. If a raw-water impeller looks perfectly fine to you, ask the mechanic to explain why he replaced it. If his explanation seems implausible, don't pay for it.

And finally, don't pay for any unauthorized work. It isn't unusual for a mechanic to say, "I know we didn't talk about it but once I got inside I thought this should be replaced." Tell him ahead of time to speak to you before he does any work you haven't already specified. Just making that statement will make him think twice about padding the work.

Most mechanics are honest, hardworking individuals, but as in every other profession there are exceptions. Armed with a working knowledge of your engine and drive, and a healthy dose of cynicism, chances are you'll never have to worry about being someone's patsy.

Basic Tools and Spare Parts

This book is specifically designed for the layman, the boat owner who prefers to leave major engine work to an expert. But even the most uninvolved owner will need to carry a few well-chosen parts and tools on board, if only to get out of a jam. The tools should fit easily into a small toolbox and the parts should take up no more than a corner of your engine compartment.

Tools

There are two ways to proceed in setting up a tool kit. You can simply go to one of the tool outlets such as Sears, get one of the 100-piece mechanic's tool kits, and keep it aboard. While it will certainly cover most of your needs, it will also cover a lot of space. Or, you can pick only those tools you think you are most likely to need. In either case, purchase good quality tools, not the kind you pull out of a bargain bin for 99 cents each. (Note that the recommendations that follow apply to your engine and stern drive only; other tools may be necessary for the rest of your boat.)

A basic tool kit should begin with a socket wrench set, from ½ to ¾ inch, along with ratchet, a couple of drive extensions, and a universal joint. You'll note that socket sets come in a variety of drive sizes and in either deep or standard socket design. You'll probably get the most use from standard-depth sockets, and find the ½-inch drive is easiest to work with and store.

In addition to socket wrenches, bring along an 8-inch adjustable wrench. Many mechanics sneer at these but they've gotten a lot of novices out of many a jam. There's nothing wrong with an adjustable

---

The Basic Tool Kit

❏ Socket wrench set, from ½-inch to ¾-inch, with ratchet, drive extensions, and a universal joint

❏ 8-inch adjustable wrench

❏ Standard pliers

❏ Needle-nosed pliers

❏ Vise-Grips

❏ Two Phillips-head screwdrivers, one extra small for tight spots

❏ Two standard (flat-head) screwdrivers, one extra small

❏ High-intensity flashlight

❏ Oil filter wrench (for canister-type fuel filters)

---

wrench as long as you buy a top-quality one. For smaller work, you might consider a nut driver, a sort of screwdriver/mini-socket wrench combo, with sockets down to at least ¼ inch.

Three pairs of pliers are a good idea: a standard pair, a pair of needle-nosed pliers, and—perhaps the most versatile tool in your kit—a pair of Vise-Grips. A pair of offset long-handle pliers (sometimes called water-pump pliers) is optional.

Pack both standard and Phillips-head screwdrivers, including an extra-small version of each, and a high-intensity flashlight designated for work only. An oil-filter wrench is a good idea if you have a canister-type fuel filter, and one especially handy item around boats is an extendable magnetic pick-up, for all those nuts and bolts you'll inevitably drop into the bilge.

This constitutes a basic tool kit, the kind needed to perform most of the basic maintenance procedures. If you're planning on more extensive work, or if you just want to be prepared for any eventuality, you may also want to include a set of combination wrenches (box- and open-end), one or two cold chisels, a prick punch, and a set of feeler gauges or an electronic dwell meter. A quick check with your local engine distributor will also get you a list of specialized tools (and a shop manual) for your type and make of engine.

If you do your boating in salt water, take steps to ensure your tools don't corrode from the salt air. Look for a toolbox with a tight-fitting lid, or better, a gasketed cover. Wipe all tools down occasionally with an oil-soaked rag to help repel moisture.

In addition to tools, you'll want a few other items in your tool kit.

Figure 18-1 If you do your boating in salt water, keep your tools in a box with a tight-fitting, gasket lid and wipe down tools with an oil-soaked rag to repel moisture and prevent corrosion.

Most important are a can of light-weight, all-purpose oil, such as WD-40, and rolls of both electrical and duct tape. A small piece of medium-grit sandpaper is handy for cleaning up metal surfaces and electrical contacts. Also include a small tube of silicone sealant, which is effective in stopping leakage and also functions well as an all-purpose adhesive. Best of all, it's easily removable.

Other items worth bringing along are an assortment of hose clamps (stainless steel only, including the bolt), and an assortment of bolts, nuts, washers, and self-tapping screws. An inexpensive circuit tester can be a big help in tracking down electrical maladies. And please don't forget that shop manual; even if you never intend to sit down and read it, you may find that some day you'll need it.

Parts

You have to make a basic philosophical decision up front regarding spare parts: Do you want to carry every conceivable part that could break during the course of a trip? Or can you be content to bring along only the essentials? If you're not likely to be more than a half-day's run from port (and parts), I suggest you conserve space and carry just the basics. These include at least one fuel filter and oil filter cartridge, at least two quarts of engine oil, and a tube of drive gear oil. Also important are one, and preferably two, raw-water pump impellers (including gaskets), a thermostat (if your boat has freshwater cooling), and an assortment of zincs.

Many boaters also bring along a set of spark plugs, a set of points, and a condenser. If you do your maintenance regularly, these and the rotor and cap shouldn't be necessary. Of course, they couldn't hurt. Remember, however, that points (and spark plugs, for that matter) are of no use if you can't set their clearance and don't have the tools to do it. Plugs don't suddenly wear out, but their insulators could break and they could become fouled if the engine fails to start.

Whatever parts you bring should be rotated into use to prevent

The Basic Parts Kit

❏   1 fuel filter

❏   1 oil filter cartridge

❏   2 quarts engine oil

❏   1 tube of gear lube

❏   1 raw-water pump impeller with gaskets

❏   1 thermostat

❏   An assortment of zincs

them from degrading in storage. For instance, if you keep an oil filter on board, the next time you change oil, use one out of your stock and replace it with a new filter. That way all of your parts will be fresh and ready for use every time you need them. Keep all your parts in water-proof containers to prevent corrosion and mildew.

Basic Engine Troubleshooting

I can't possibly give you specific instructions on how to fix your stern drive engine. Any attempt at that would be futile, if for no other reason than even within the same brand, each model is slightly different from the other. Comprehensive troubleshooting instructions would be either prohibitively long or so vague as to be useless.

Instead I'll concentrate on a brief philosophical discussion about the art of troubleshooting, and I'll give you a few basic questions to ask yourself before you call a mechanic. If you're looking for something more specific, purchase the shop manual for your particular engine. Most include a comprehensive troubleshooting chart that can walk you through virtually any problem.

Despite the vast array of sophisticated testing equipment available, your senses remain your most valuable diagnostic tools; odd sounds or odors, hot surfaces, or the color of the engine's exhaust can announce problems long before they appear on gauges.

Get to know the sound of your engine. When you hear something out of the ordinary, pay attention. A loud knocking, for instance, could signal a bad connecting rod—or just an engine hatch left ajar. A strong odor could indicate a fuel leak, an overheating engine, or an electrical problem. You often can locate the source of an overheating problem by feeling—with extreme caution—for hot and cold spots.

Your eyes can be helpful as well. One of the best ways to tell how an engine is running is by the color of its exhaust, an accurate diagnostic technique when used with certain limitations in mind. Remember that because a marine engine mixes water with its exhaust, the exhaust is more difficult to read than an automotive engine's.

Two exhaust colors indicate problems: black and blue. Black exhaust indicates either too much fuel or not enough air. Two possible explanations for black exhaust could be either a clogged air intake or an improperly adjusted fuel system. Blue smoke indicates that oil is burning in the combustion chamber. Possible causes here could be worn piston rings or cylinder walls, worn valve guides, or a clogged crankcase ventilator. If your engine is emitting blue smoke, the first step should be to check the engine log for indications of unusual oil consumption. If that is indicated, the next step is a compression check of each cylinder.

The Troubleshooting Process

Troubleshooting is really nothing more than a logical process of elimination, but to do it well you must have at least a basic knowledge of how an engine works. If you've read this book, you know enough about a stern drive engine to troubleshoot it. Here are three simple questions to ask that probably will unearth almost any problem:

1. Have I Done All the Simple Things? If you remember only one lesson from this chapter, this is the one to remember: Your engine is basically reliable and durable, and it's unlikely that it will ever actually break. More often, the problem will be that you have overlooked some minor detail that has caused the engine to malfunction. There is an unalterable human desire to find a macro reason for a problem, when more often it's just a micro glitch that's put you out of service. Think small.

For instance, suppose your engine simply stops running. Before you suspect that the crankshaft has broken in two, walk yourself back through the most basic steps in starting. Is the key on? (Yes, you turned it on, but has it been turned off inadvertently?) Is the safety lanyard in place? Is there fuel in the tank? (The gauge says there is, but are you sure the fuel gauge is accurate or even working?) Is the fuel getting from the tank to the engine? (Did you remember to turn the fuel valve back on after you changed the filter?)

The key here is always to look at the most basic (and therefore the least likely) cause for a problem. Resist the urge to pick up a tool or call a mechanic. Don't panic. Think logically and sequentially. In the majority of cases, you'll find the culprit is not-so-obvious but so simple as to be truly embarrassing.

2. Has Anything Changed? If your engine ran fine yesterday but shows no signs of life today, ask yourself if anything has been done in the interim. Have you put fuel in it? If so, maybe the fuel is contaminated. Have you or a mechanic worked on it? If the answer is yes, resist the most common step, which is to say, "But that couldn't have anything to do with it."

For instance, suppose your stern drive refuses to start, but it started fine yesterday. The only thing that happened over the last 24 hours is that you changed the oil. But how could an oil change cause an engine to quit? Retrace your steps in the engine room and you may find that you inadvertently nudged a fuel valve closed or knocked a wire loose.

3. *Does the Engine Have Fuel and Electricity?* Suppose you've asked yourself the first two questions and the answers have not revealed a solution. Now it's time to look deeper for a solution. First, make sure your engine has what it needs. If you've read this book you know that means clean fuel and air, and a supply of electricity. As you ask these questions, start once again with the simplest explanations first and progress in a logical, orderly manner.

Any good mechanic knows there are four basic diagnostic tests to run on a four-cycle gasoline engine that will almost always reveal the source of the problem. They are:

- Check for spark. If the engine won't turn over, you know your problem is probably on the 12-volt side, and it's probably a dead battery. If is does turn over, your next step is to check for spark. The easiest way to do this is to just pull a spark plug, attach the spark plug wire, ground the threads of the spark plug to metal (preferably on the engine block), and have someone crank the engine. You should be able to tell immediately if there's spark. If there isn't, likely culprits are points and condenser or an electronic ignition module.

- Check the condition of the spark plug. If it's wet with fuel you know fuel is getting to the combustion chamber. If it's dry, you may have a fuel supply problem. If the plug is really wet, you've probably flooded the engine. First try to start it with the throttle wide open, which will admit more air. If that doesn't work, pull all the plugs, wipe them clean, and if possible, regap them.

- Check the carburetor. Your next step is to make sure fuel is getting to the carburetor. Remove the flame arrestor. Unplug the lead from the coil to the distributor so the engine won't start. Look into the carburetor and quickly open the throttle all the way—you can usually do this right at the carburetor by just grabbing the linkage. You should see the accelerator pump shoot raw gas right into the venturi. (If you can't see it, you should at least smell it.) If you can't, chances are no fuel is getting to the carburetor. Likely explanations are empty fuel tank, clogged fuel filter, or a clogged anti-siphon valve where the fuel line meets the tank. Remove this valve with your adjustable wrench, blow it out, and re-insert it.

- Check the compression. If the simple checks fail to reveal the solution, you may have a serious problem. It's time to check the compression with a compression gauge. Low compression is a sign of a broken piston ring, burned valve, or even a cracked cylinder head.

Overheating

One final problem you may someday have to troubleshoot is overheating. Again, the key is to proceed sequentially. First, is water coming into the boat past the water intakes on the drive? Believe it or not, many overheating problems are the result of nothing more than a plastic bag wrapped around the drive unit.

Second, is the raw-water pump functioning? (Is the exhaust pipe cool downstream of the exhaust elbow? If freshwater-cooled, is there sufficient coolant in the engine? (**Don't remove the cap!** Check the coolant recovery bottle or wait until the engine cools.)

There are literally thousands more questions you could ask in your quest to find the gremlin in your engine. Whatever your predicament, the key is to proceed slowly and logically. Never skip a step. If you can't find the problem by an orderly, sequential process of elimination, then chances are you have a fairly serious problem. That means it's time to quit playing detective and call in an expert.

Index

Additives, cooling system, 44; fuel, 4, 66; oil, 25–26, 60
Air pollution, 9
Alcohol in fuel, 64
Anodes. *See* Zincs
Antifreeze, 44, 48

Backfiring, 12
Batteries, 48, 67
Bearings, 4
Belts, 50
Blowers, bilge, 54
Bonding, electrical, 35
Breaker points. *See* Points

Camshafts, 6
Carburetors, 9–14
Cathodes, 35
Cavitation, 33
Checklists, 38–53
Chokes, 12–14
Clutches, dog, 29–31; cone, 31–32
Combustion chambers, 3
Compression ratio, 3
Condenser, 16
Connecting rod, 4
Coolant. *See* Antifreeze
Cooling, exhaust, 22

Cooling, freshwater, 21, 44, 48, 50
Cooling systems, 5, 19–21
Corrosion, 21, 34, 73
Crankshafts, 4
Cylinder heads, 2

Distributor, 15, 68
Drive train, 27–35
Dwell meter, 68

Electrical systems, 15–18, 45, 48, 49
Electrolysis, 34
Exhaust systems, 22–24; bypass, 23

Feeler gauge, 17, 72
Filters, air, 10; fuel, 9, 65, 72; oil, 50, 62, 71
Flame arrestor, 10, 73
Fuel consumption, 56
Fuel systems, 9–14, 49, 64–66

Gauges, 41, 44, 83
Gears, 27, 54

Hoses, 49
Hour meter, 39
Hydraulic systems, 28, 32, 73, 74
Hydrometer, 48

Ignition systems, 15–18, 67–69, 72; electronic, 16; advance, 17

Kick-up systems, 32
Knocking, 64

Logs, 38–42
Longevity, 54, 60
Lubrication systems, 5, 25–26, 33, 43–44, 47, 51

Maintenance, 38–42
Mercury Marine, 18, 32, 33, 34, 54
Moisture, in fuel, 64, 66; in ignition systems, 67

Oil, 60–63; changing of, 70, 74; consumption, 41; viscosity, 61. *See also* Lubrication systems
Outboard Marine Corporation (OMC), 13, 20, 24, 26, 30, 31, 32, 33, 51, 55

Parts, spare, 80–81
Pistons, 2
Points, 16, 68
Pollution, 9
Propellers, 33, 34, 57
Pumps, accelerator, 14, 57, 84; fuel, 9; power steering, 73; water, 19

Records, 38–42

Repairs and servicing, 75–77
Rust. *See* Corrosion

Salt water, 15, 23, 74, 79
Sea cocks, 49
Smoke, 83
Spark advance, 17
Spark plugs, 4, 17–18, 69; wires, 67–68
Speed, 56
Steering, 27, 33, 73
Stern drive units, 27–35, 63

Tanks, fuel, 66
Thermostats, 20
Tools, 78–80
Trim tabs, 33, 56
Troubleshooting, 82–85

Universal joints, 28

Valves, 6
V-belts, 50
Ventilation, propeller, 33
Volvo Penta, 28, 32, 33, 34

Wake, 56
Wear, engine, 56
Weather, 42

Yamaha, 3, 23, 33

Zincs, 21, 34, 50, 52, 74